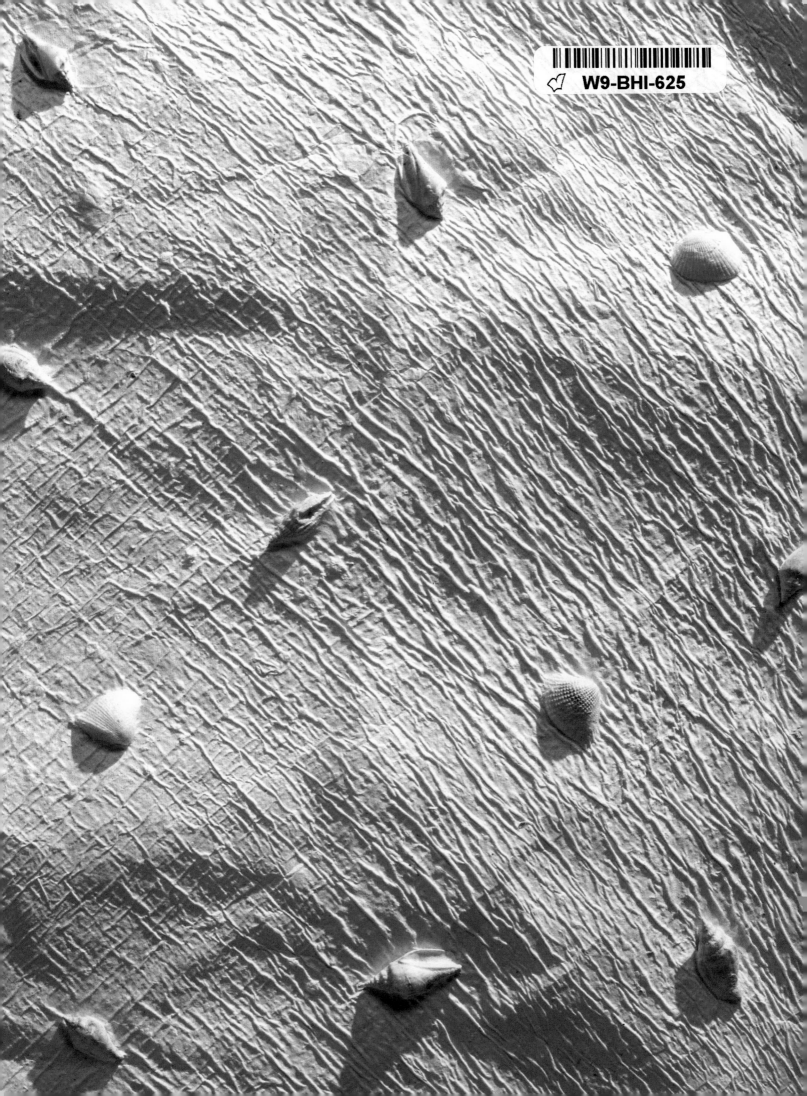

PAPERCRAFT

of the World

PAPERCRAFT

of the World

THUNDER BAY
P·R·E·S·S

First published in the United States 1995
by Thunder Bay Press
5880 Oberlin Drive, Suite 400, San Diego, CA 92121-9653

Copyright © 1995 WORLD LIVING ARTS Pty Limited

Publisher: Tracy Marsh
Art Director: Vicki James
Project Coordinator: Debi McCulloch
Editor: Susan Gray
Editorial Assistant: Leonie Draper
Graphic Designer: Peta Nugent
Photographer: Adam Bruzzone
Photographic Stylist: Anne-Maree Unwin
Production Manager: Mick Bagnato

Library of Congress Cataloging-in-Publication Data
Papercraft of the world / [editor. Susan Gray].
     p.   cm.
  "First published in Australia in 1995 by RD Press" --T.p. verso.
  Includes index.
  ISBN 1-57145-065-3
  1. Paper work. 2. Paper. Handmade.   I. Gray, Susan. 1967-
TT870.P365 1995
745.54--dc20   95-18366
                                                          CIP

Manufactured by Mandarin Offset, Hong Kong
Printed in Hong Kong

CONTENTS

About this book ✦ *6*

PAPER MAKING ✦ *8*

MEXICAN PAPERCRAFT ✦ *28*

MARBLING ✦ *38*

DÉCOUPAGE ✦ *54*

JAPANESE PAPERCRAFT ✦ *66*

PAPIER-MÂCHÉ ✦ *82*

PAPER CUTTING ✦ *94*

QUILLING ✦ *106*

CHINESE PAPERCRAFT ✦ *114*

GENERAL INFORMATION ✦ *128*

 Paper types

 Materials

 Techniques

 Making equipment

 Patterns

Glossary ✦ *172*

Contributors ✦ *174*

Index ✦ *175*

Acknowledgements ✦ *176*

ABOUT THIS BOOK

PAPER RANKS AS ONE OF civilization's greatest inventions. The implications of the discovery of this fragile material have been extraordinarily far-reaching, with paper having become an essential item in the daily lives of almost all people around the world. As a creative medium, paper is versatile, and its low cost and abundance has made it one of the most popular of all craft materials.

This book focuses on nine papercrafts, each belonging to a separate tradition. These traditions are defined either by cultural groupings, wherein papercrafts display distinctive features; or by styles, which cross national boundaries and belong to many cultures. Paper

Quilled posy was first invented in the East, and although its spread to the West, and then to the remainder of the world, did not begin until nearly one thousand years later, the delay did nothing to prevent papercraft traditions from becoming firmly entrenched in places as far removed as Poland and Pennsylvania, Mexico and the Mediterranean.

The versatility of paper is one reason for its popularity. It can be used wet, as with paper making and papier-mâché, or dry, as with paper cutting and kite making. It can be layered to make découpage pieces, folded to form origami shapes, rolled to create quilled designs, incised to reveal cut paper images, or simply used in sheet form to pick up a marbled print. This book allows

you to sample a wide variety of papercrafts and encourages further exploration of those crafts which interest you most.

Each chapter reviews a different paper tradition. The chapter opening page provides insight into the history of each style, while the traditional and modern papercraft ideas presented in the Designs and Variations spreads offer inspiration for adapting designs and for ways of approaching other paper projects. Each project then guides you, step-by-step, through the stages needed to produce a papercraft item. The projects are graded in the following way:

BEGINNER
No experience required, but you will need to refer to the General Information chapter

INTERMEDIATE
Requires some practice or knowledge of the techniques before undertaking the project

ADVANCED
Includes some difficult steps, but with patience can be successfully completed

The General Information section at the back of the book contains advice on materials, techniques and tools. A chart, showing the different types of paper used in making the projects, explains the distinctive qualities of each material. This is followed by a detailed explanation of some of the techniques touched upon in the main text, plus an illustrated description of how to make a few simple papercrafting tools. Patterns to scale, a comprehensive glossary, a brief biography of each of the contributors, and an index to help you locate information, complete *Papercrafts of the World.*

In Mexico, many paper items are still made by hand. Here an artisan is making papel picado *for a traditional celebration.*

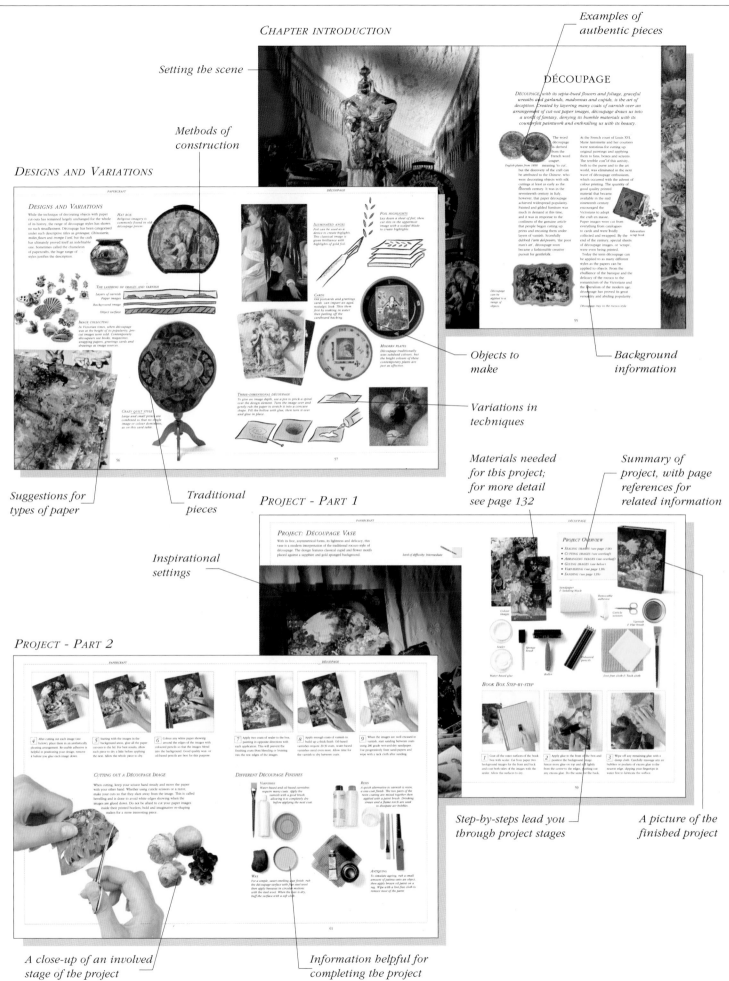

CHAPTER INTRODUCTION

Setting the scene

Examples of
authentic pieces

Methods of
construction

DESIGNS AND VARIATIONS

Objects to
make

Background
information

Variations in
techniques

Materials needed
for this project;
for more detail
see page 132

Summary of
project, with page
references for
related information

Suggestions for
types of paper

Traditional
pieces

PROJECT - PART 1

Inspirational
settings

PROJECT - PART 2

Step-by-steps lead you
through project stages

A picture of the
finished project

A close-up of an involved
stage of the project

Information helpful for
completing the project

PAPER MAKING

THE TACTILE QUALITIES of handmade paper make its manufacture and use a sensuous experience, but Eastern and Western expectations of this ephemeral product have long diverged. Although paper making has two distinct traditions, the fine and unique materials which result from both of them have ensured an enduring appreciation of the craft.

Handmade stationery

Silk, bamboo, *amate*, papyrus and parchment have all been used to preserve information, but it was the process of pulping vegetable fibers and collecting them on a framed screen that revolutionized written communications. Discovered by the Chinese almost two thousand years ago, the technique enabled macerated hemp, rags and fishing nets to be transformed into paper. As the technology spread through Asia it was discovered that barks, leaves and grasses produced thin, pliant papers of very high quality.

The needs of Western paper users were, however, different from those of the East. When paper making reached Europe along the trade routes, almost a millennium after it was discovered in the East, new properties were demanded of the material.

Whereas in the East, paper had been revered as almost sacred and the secrets of its production kept closely guarded, the West, with its printing presses and insatiable appetite for banknotes, certificates and receipts, insisted that paper be white, opaque and, above all, uniform in size and texture.

Ultimately the pulping process came under the domain of the machine. The Hollander Beater was designed in the seventeenth century to refine the cotton and linen rags, hemp rope and sail cloth which initially provided the raw materials for western paper making.

A shortage of these fabrics precipitated the change of source material and the complete mechanization of paper making. In 1806, wood pulp was fed into the first Fourdrinier machine. Henceforth, uniform paper could be produced in a continuous web.

Despite the mechanization of the paper making process, or perhaps because of it, the beauty and individuality of a sheet of hand-made paper remain unsurpassed.

Boxes covered with leaf-embedded paper

Sheets of paper dry on wooden racks in a paper making workshop.

Papers made with dyed and seeded pulp

DESIGNS AND VARIATIONS

Paper making has two traditions; the first is distinguished by the fine aesthetic qualities of its product, while the papers of the second are notable for their functionality. The differences between Eastern and Western paper making traditions can be partially accounted for by raw materials, writing implements and printing processes. But paper making techniques remain largely the same, reminding us of the common history uniting the two.

PLANT FIBERS
Ordinary vegetables such as leeks and celery can be macerated and used as fiber pulp for making paper.

PAPER PULP
Functional objects can be made by combining shredded paper with water and pressing the pulp into a mold.

FLOWERS
Pressed pansies, forget-me-nots and other flowers can be added to the paper pulp in the vat to make beautiful floral papers.

WATERMARKS
Fine wires sewn onto the screen of a mold create translucent images in a sheet of paper, guaranteeing the quality of the handmade product.

10

PAPER PRODUCTS

Tote bags, albums and gift wrap - just some of the items that can be produced from handmade paper.

BINDING

Most books are printed on machine-made paper, but handmade papers can also be bound to make distinctive books.

EMBEDDING

Threads, flowers, leaves and shells can be incorporated into a piece of paper prior to couching.

PROJECT: MAKING PAPER

Fibers of flax run through this handmade paper, providing it with its
essential strength and giving it a beautiful, textured finish. Mountboard,
available from picture framers as scrap, is used to make the quality
recycled pulp that comprises the bulk of the paper.

Level of difficulty: Beginner

PROJECT OVERVIEW

- *PREPARING PULP (see page 134)*
- *FILLING VAT (see below)*
- *MAKING EQUIPMENT (see page 142)*
- *SHEET FORMING (see overleaf)*
- *COUCHING (see page 135)*
- *DRYING SHEETS (see page 15)*

Blender

Couching pad:
Felt, Boards &
Cotton fabric

Mountboard
& Scrap paper

Pulped flax

Vat

Roller

C-clamps

Mold &
Deckle

Water pitcher

MAKING PAPER STEP-BY-STEP

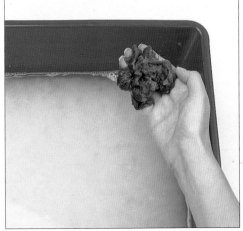

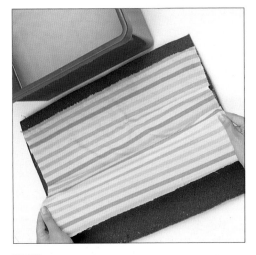

1 Tear enough mountboard and paper to half-fill a bucket and soak for 24 hours. Place a handful of the paper into a blender, add water to the three-quarter mark and blend to a creamy pulp. Blend all the paper in this manner.

2 Fill the vat three-quarters full with water. Add two or three pitchers of paper pulp plus a handful of prepared fiber pulp (see page 135). This paper uses flax, but other fibers are suitable (see page 18). Stir the contents of the vat.

3 Prepare the couching pad in readiness for transferring sheets of paper from the mold. Lay down a wooden board slightly larger than the size of your mold. Lay a square of thick felt on top, then a piece of damp cotton fabric.

4   Lower the mold and deckle into the vat, scoop through the pulp in a downwards sweeping motion and lift directly up and out of the vat. Shake the frame from side to side then top to bottom to interlace the fibers. Allow to drain.

5   Remove the deckle. Press one edge of the mold vertically against the couching pad. Lower it onto the pad. Apply pressure evenly to the frame while rocking it gently back and forth. Lift it away from the sheet by tilting up and to one side.

6   Place a damp cotton cloth over the paper. Smooth the couching sheet to avoid wrinkles in the paper. Continue sheet-forming, layering each piece of paper between damp cloths. Add more pulp to the vat as the fiber content decreases.

DIPPING THE MOLD & DECKLE

The action for collecting the pulp on the screen is the most important one in the paper making process. If the mold and deckle are not lowered and lifted smoothly, the pulp will settle unevenly. The two parts of the frame should be held firmly and lowered from a vertical position above the vat to a horizontal position underneath the liquid's surface. The mold should be at a slight angle as it breaks through the surface into the pulp mixture, then held flat as it is raised up and out of the pulp.

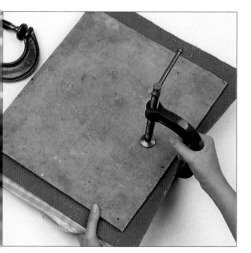

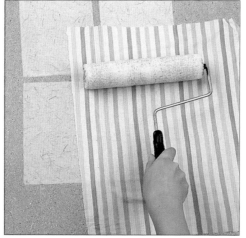

7 Cover the last couching sheet with a square of felt and then a piece of board. Several sheets of paper should lie between the pressing boards. Attach clamps to the boards, tighten, and tilt the boards to one side to allow the water to drain away.

8 When drained, remove the clamps and lift off the top couching sheet. The paper will remain attached to it. Lay the sheet, with the paper side downwards, on a smooth surface such as glass or wood. Use a roller to press the paper flat.

9 Separate the couching sheet from the paper by gently lifting one corner of the couching sheet away from the drying surface, using your finger to hold the paper to the board. Remove the fabric and leave the paper to dry for 24 hours.

SIZING PAPER

Sizing makes paper stonger and less absorbent. Papers that are to be used for writing or painting benefit from the application of a size coating. Several kinds of size are available; some are added to the pulp in the vat, while others are applied with a brush or sponge to the dried sheets. The latter method works best on papers that have been dried, or seasoned, for at least two weeks. (See page 135 for more information on sizing.)

HERCON

A non-toxic, professional size. Mix ⅓ oz (10 ml) per bucket of pulp, plus two teaspoons of baking soda. Add to the pulp in the vat.

GELATIN

A good homemade size. Dissolve 4 tsp or ⅔ oz of gelatin into 4 cups or 32 fl oz or 1 qt of boiling water. Pour into the vat or spray onto seasoned paper.

COMMERCIAL STARCH

The quickest method of sizing. Spray directly onto seasoned paper and leave to dry, then repeat twice more.

CORNSTARCH

Made from the standard pantry product. Mix 1⅔ oz (50 ml) of cornstarch with 12⅓ fl oz (350 ml) of warm water to make a smooth liquid. Pour into the vat and make paper as usual.

METHYL CELLULOSE

A versatile size available from hardware stores. Mix ¼ oz (7 ml) of methyl cellulose with a little water to make a thick jelly, then add 1 qt (1 l) of water. Add to the vat, or spray onto paper.

PROJECT: STATIONERY BOX

One of the most appealing qualities of handmade paper is its texture.
This project celebrates the beauty of handmade paper. It is constructed
by making two open boxes and attaching them to a hinged cover so
that they fit inside each other when the cover is closed.

Level of difficulty: Advanced

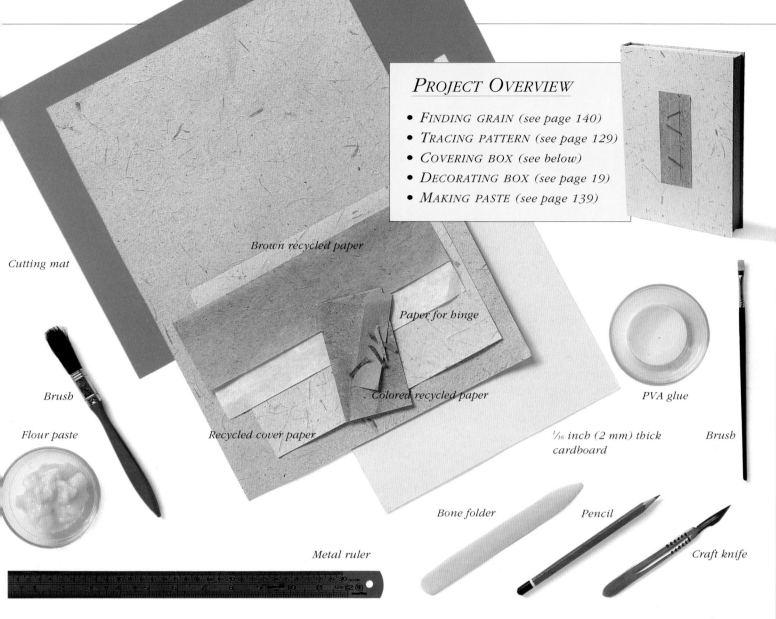

PROJECT OVERVIEW

- FINDING GRAIN (see page 140)
- TRACING PATTERN (see page 129)
- COVERING BOX (see below)
- DECORATING BOX (see page 19)
- MAKING PASTE (see page 139)

Brown recycled paper

Cutting mat

Paper for hinge

Brush

Colored recycled paper

PVA glue

Flour paste

Recycled cover paper

¹⁄₁₆ inch (2 mm) thick cardboard

Brush

Bone folder

Pencil

Metal ruler

Craft knife

STATIONERY BOX STEP-BY-STEP

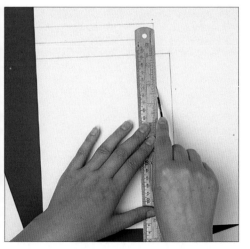

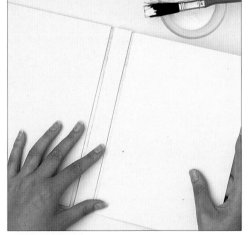

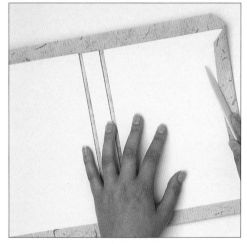

1 Transfer the outside cover pieces (pattern page 148) onto cardboard. Ensure that the grain of each piece lies in the same direction; cut out precisely. The front and back pieces are slightly different in size, so it is a good idea to label them.

2 Measure and cut a 15¾ x 11½ inch (40 x 29 cm) piece of paper for the cover. Also cut the paper for hinge and mark the lines where indicated on the pattern. Paste the hinge paper to the spine boards at the pencil marks, then paste to the cover.

3 Trim each of the four corners of the cover paper, on the diagonal, to a point ¹⁄₁₆ inch (2 mm) out from the cardboard corners. Apply paste to the paper and fold it over, making creases with a bone folder and pressing firmly to secure.

4 Trace and cut the brown recycled paper piece and apply paste to one side of it. Position over the inside spine so that it overlaps the front and back covers by an equal distance. Use a bone folder to press the paper into the hinge grooves.

5 Trace and cut the cardboard pieces for the boxes. Apply glue to the ¹⁄₁₆ inch (2 mm) wide cut edge of each long side strip and place perpendicularly against the long edge of each of the box bases. Glue the two sides of each short strip and press in place.

6 Collect the cover papers for the boxes. Apply paste to the surface of one of the short side pieces. Working on the front box, press the edge indicated on the pattern piece to the underneath side of the box, then smooth the paper around the outside.

FIBERS SUITABLE FOR PAPER MAKING

The leaves and stems of numerous long-fibered plants can be used to make paper. Shown below are fibers which the home paper maker can easily process by boiling and beating. (See page 135 for instructions.) The papers shown on the left, from top to bottom, are made from the leaves of the pineapple, yucca and banana.

BANANA LEAVES
Macerate the leaves while they are still green, or allow them to dry in the sun first.

YUCCA LEAVES
Strip off the tough outer skin of the leaves before processing them.

PINEAPPLE TOPS
The stiff leaves found at the top of the pineapple make a pulp which produces an almost transparent paper.

18

7 Continue smoothing the paper to the inside of the box. Press the small flaps around, one to cover the inside corner, the other to cover the outside corner. Cover the other short side of the front box, then both short sides of the back box, in the same way.

8 Cover the long side of both boxes. Apply paste to each cover strip and press to the underneath side of each box. Smooth the paper up and over the rim, then press to the inside base. Paste the base cover papers to the inside base of each box.

9 Brush glue onto the back of the smaller (front) box and attach it to the inside left flap of the cover. Attach the larger (back) box to the right cover. Close the lid to check that the boxes fit inside one another. Press with heavy books until dry.

DECORATING THE STATIONERY BOX

Select colorful scraps of recycled paper and cut them into shapes to decorate the cover of your stationery box. Fix in place according to your own sense of design, using paste.

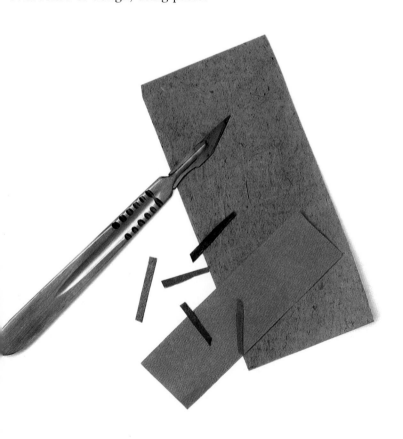

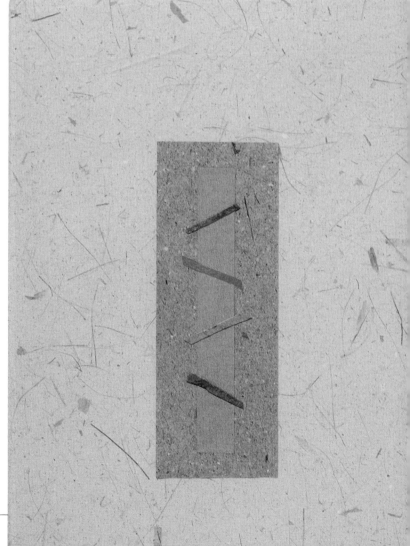

PROJECT: HANDMADE PAPER BOOK

In past centuries, the crisp white paper familiar to us today was much coveted, but now the handmade product is gaining in appeal. Use the paper you produced in the first project, or any handmade paper, to make an attractive and practical book from recycled paper.

Level of difficulty: Intermediate

PROJECT OVERVIEW

- *TEARING PAPER (see page 140)*
- *MAKING COVER (see below)*
- *FORMING PAGES (see overleaf)*
- *BINDING (see overleaf)*
- *GLUING ENDPAPERS (see page 23)*

Cardboard

Glue

Strong thread & Needle

Craft knife

Pencil

Metal ruler   *Brush*

Handmade paper

BOOK STEP-BY-STEP

1 Mark two rectangles, each 6½ x 4½ inches (165 x 115 mm), and one strip, 6½ x ½ inches (165 x 13 mm), on cardboard. Cut the pieces out against a metal ruler, using a craft knife and working on a mat.

2 Center the cardboard on a sheet of handmade paper. Use a pencil to lightly mark the corner positions. Brush glue onto the cardboard and press into place, using the pencil markings as guides.

3 Diagonally trim each of the corners of the paper to about 1/16 inch (2 mm) out from the corners of the cardboard. Apply glue to the paper and fold it over onto the cardboard. Press firmly until the glue dries.

4 Take the five sheets reserved for the pages, fold each in half and tear along the crease. Fold these torn sheets in half, re-open and bundle them together in threes. (One sheet will remain unused.)

5 Along the fold line of each sheaf, mark two points at one- and two-third intervals. Insert a threaded needle from the outside at one marked point and push it back out through the other point.

6 Place the next sheaf alongside the sewn one and repeat the binding process. Do this again with the third and last sheaf. Tie the ends of the thread together in a firm knot. Trim excess thread.

TEXTURAL EFFECTS

By adding various materials to the vat before forming the sheets, or by impressing fibers into a newly formed sheet while it is still on the mold, some fascinating textural effects are possible. The first method is the more random, while pressing fibers directly onto the pulp on the mold allows greater control over the design.

LEAVES

The tips of conifer leaves are dried and sealed with PVA glue, then carefully arranged in rows on the paper while it is on the mold.

REEDS

Reeds are laid along the vertical and horizontal lengths of the pulp on the mold after most of the water has drained away.

WHEAT HUSKS

Dry wheat husks are added to the vat with paper pulp and strained through the mesh of the mold.

7 Brush glue along the inside spine of the cover and position the bound pages against the glue. Make sure the ends of the thread are invisible. Hold in position until the glue dries.

8 For the endpapers, fold a sheet of letter paper in half and tear. Fold both pieces in half again. Apply glue to both the inside cover and the first page and press the endpaper in place. Repeat for the back.

PUTTING THE BOOK TOGETHER

The thread which binds the book together remains visible at the center page of each sheaf. It is possible to make a feature of this by using brightly colored threads, or by knotting the thread on the inside rather than at the spine. Similarly, endpapers can reflect your taste. Use marbled paper or wrapping paper, or simply use plain paper which contrasts with the cover paper. The variations are limitless.

PROJECT: PAPER PULP BOWL

Paper pulping differs from papier-mâché in that it does not require glue and is a much quicker way of building up thickness than layering. By pressing differently colored pulps into a bowl lined with strands of wool, a striking contemporary bowl can be made.

Level of difficulty: Beginner

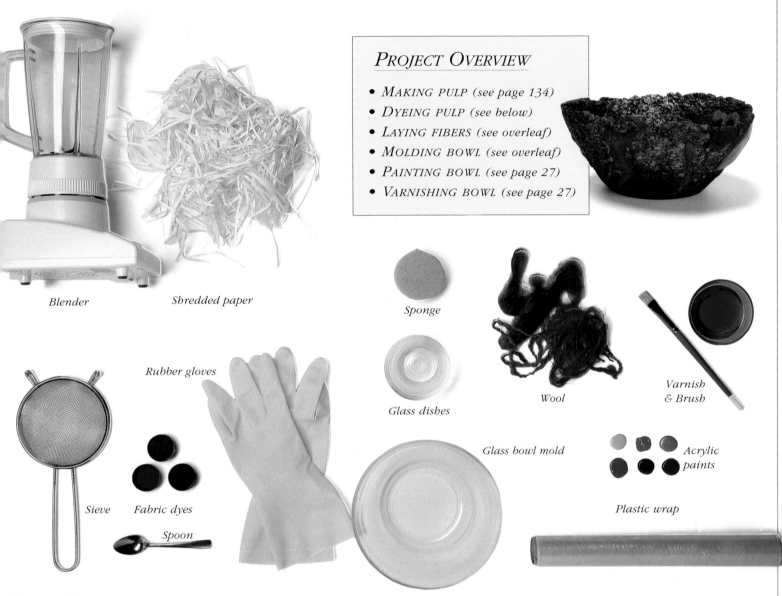

Blender

Shredded paper

PROJECT OVERVIEW

- *MAKING PULP (see page 134)*
- *DYEING PULP (see below)*
- *LAYING FIBERS (see overleaf)*
- *MOLDING BOWL (see overleaf)*
- *PAINTING BOWL (see page 27)*
- *VARNISHING BOWL (see page 27)*

Sponge

Rubber gloves

Wool

Varnish & Brush

Glass dishes

Sieve   Fabric dyes

Glass bowl mold

Acrylic paints

Spoon

Plastic wrap

BOWL STEP-BY-STEP

1 Soak the shredded paper in a bucket of water for 24 hours. Place small amounts of the softened paper in a blender with water and blend it until it is reduced to pulp. Remove excess water by straining the pulp through a sieve.

2 Divide the strained pulp into three parts and place in separate glass dishes ready for dyeing. Wearing rubber gloves, add powdered fabric dyes to each of the pulps, stirring thoroughly. Follow the manufacturer's instructions for using dyes.

3 Individually return each of the colored pulps to the sieve and rinse in cold water under a tap until the water runs clear. This is to prevent the different colors from running into one another once pressed into the mold.

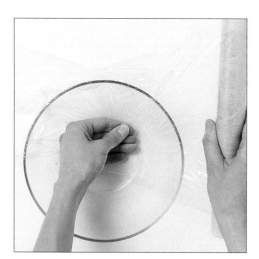

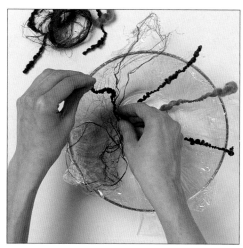

4 Choose a mold that is wider at the top than at the bottom. Line with plastic wrap so that the pulp will not stick to the glass and the dried pulp bowl can be removed from the mold.

5 Select materials to be embedded into the pulp. This example uses strands of wool, but a range of other materials can be used (see below). Lay the fibers evenly around the inside of the bowl.

6 Cover the fibers with the pulp, removing any excess water with a sponge. Press the pulp into the shape of the bowl to a thickness of about ½ inch (10 mm). Leave to dry in a warm place.

MATERIALS TO BE EMBEDDED INTO PULP

The range of items that can be embedded into paper pulp is almost unlimited. Materials which have a textured surface tend to interlace with the paper fibers better. Choose items that are not too bulky.

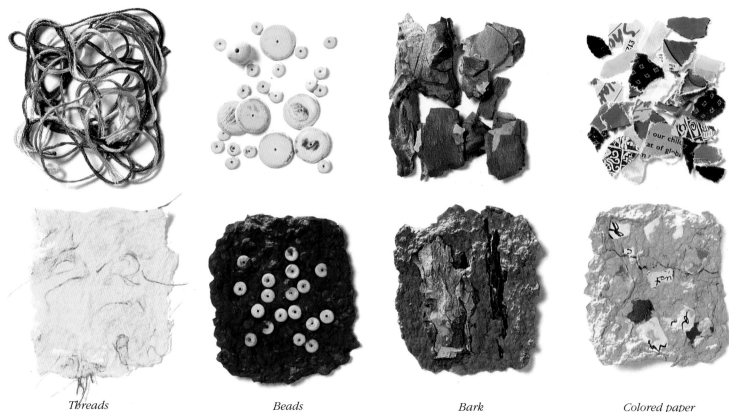

Threads   *Beads*   *Bark*   *Colored paper*

7 When dry, the paper pulp bowl will have shrunk a little, allowing it to be easily removed from the mold. Carefully peel the plastic wrap from the pulp bowl. Allow it more time to dry fully.

8 Paint highlights onto the bowl using acrylic paints. Choose colors that complement those of the dyes and wools, brushing the paints on as you desire. Add the final highlights in gold metallic paint.

9 When the paints have dried, apply several coats of clear varnish to the inside and outside of the bowl to make it sturdy and water-resistant. Allow time for the varnish to dry between coats.

Dried flowers   *Wool*   *Leaves and ferns*   *Dyed burlap*

MEXICAN PAPERCRAFT

FROM COLORFUL PAPERCUTS fluttering on strings outside village churches, to poles laden with grinning papier-mâché figures, the impact of paper is visible everywhere in Mexico today. Introduced by the Spanish conquistadors in 1519, paper has pervaded almost every arena of Mexican daily life, so much so that it is easy to forget its foreign and relatively recent origins.

Papercuts of amate *paper*

Although paper as we know it was imported to Mexico, another primitive paper made from bark was in use from Aztec times. Called *amate*, this paper served as a magic ingredient in many pagan rituals. Mulberry trees provided a white paper that could appease the gods, while black paper, made from the bark of fig trees, could invoke evil spirits. White paper figures were often pinned over doors to ward off black magic.

It was, however, with the introduction of European papers that papercrafts flowered. *Papel picado*, the craft of perforating layers of tissue and metallic paper with a chisel, is practiced widely in Mexico today. The bright, lacy papercuts are strung up outside churches for festive occasions such as weddings and saints' days.

Colorful, lacy papel picado decorate a lively cathedral square.

During Holy Week celebrations, grotesque papier-mâché figures called *Judases* also adorn village squares. Representing devils, skeletons and other grimly comical creatures, *Judases* are filled with fireworks and exploded to the sound of jeers and laughter.

Alebridges, fantastical creatures modelled in papier-mâché, are a testament to the whimsical spirit of their Mexican makers. These toys are designed for the amusement of children and adults alike. *Piñatas*, by contrast, are purposely made for the young. These fanciful creations take the form of stars, fish, donkeys and other animals and are made out of paper. They hold pots full of candy and toys which spill out over the crowd when a blindfolded child wielding a stick breaks open the suspended toy.

Piñata *bull*

Mexico is renowned for the fluency with which elements of the new and the old are combined. The beautiful and original paper creations made by its craftspeople today are a tribute to the nation's vigor, style and delight in the unusual.

Detail of a papier-mâché alebridge

DESIGNS AND VARIATIONS

Mexican design has had a long evolution, dating back at least one thousand years before Christ. The Olmecs, Mayas, Toltecs and Aztecs all contributed creative elements, but it was the Spanish who perhaps bestowed most to the Mexican craft heritage. With the skills they had acquired from the Moors, the Spanish brought new techniques and materials to Mexico. Amongst these, paper was one of the most significant.

BIRD OF PARADISE
A colorful detail from a painting on bark.

DOLLS
Painted papier-mâché dolls bring pleasure to their makers as much as to those who receive them.

MASKS
Papier-mâché masks are part of the Day of the Dead celebrations.

COLOR
The rainbow is the Mexican palette, as attested to by the vivid colors of these paper flowers.

BARK PAINTING
Scenes of daily life are painted onto amate *paper, made from the bark of mulberry trees.*

PAPEL PICADO
Papercut images recall departed souls on the Day of the Dead. Sharp blades are hammered through layers of colored tissue paper to make the lacy decorations.

ALEBRIDGES
The mystical Mexican imagination is responsible for fabulous beasts made from papier-mâché.

AMATE
Cut-outs of a paper made from bark were believed by native Indians to improve crop yields.

JUDASES
Representations of devils, despots and politicians made from papier-mâché are ritually burned on Holy Saturday.

Project: Mexican Piñata

A typical feature of the Christmas season in Mexico are the colorful *piñatas*. Made to be broken, these papier-mâché creations are filled with candy and small toys which shower down upon the blindfolded child who successfully breaks the suspended *piñata* with a stick.

Level of difficulty: Intermediate

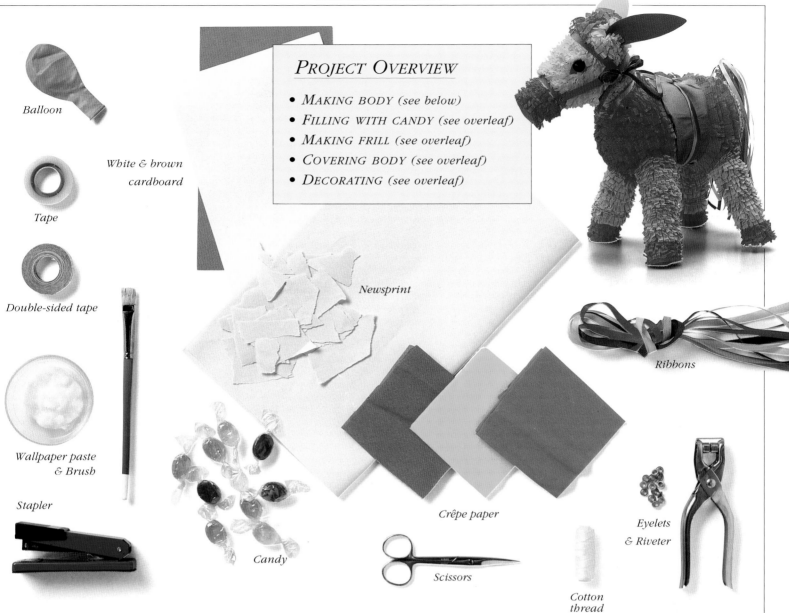

Balloon

Tape

Double-sided tape

White & brown cardboard

PROJECT OVERVIEW

- MAKING BODY (see below)
- FILLING WITH CANDY (see overleaf)
- MAKING FRILL (see overleaf)
- COVERING BODY (see overleaf)
- DECORATING (see overleaf)

Newsprint

Ribbons

Wallpaper paste & Brush

Stapler

Candy

Crêpe paper

Scissors

Cotton thread

Eyelets & Riveter

PIÑATA *STEP-BY-STEP*

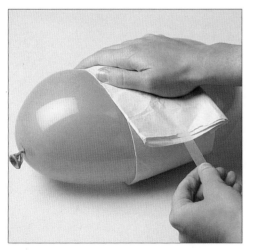

1 Inflate a balloon to the size of a basketball or slightly larger. Flatten the center of the ball to elongate the shape by securing a long, folded piece of newsprint around its center with tape.

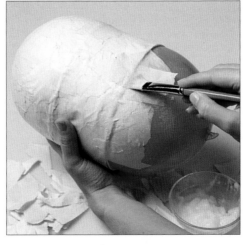

2 Apply no more than five or six layers of papier-mâché over the balloon using torn pieces of paper and wallpaper paste. Do not cover the knot of the balloon as you will need to remove it later.

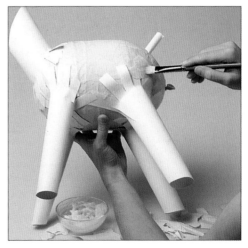

3 Cut the pieces for the neck, legs and tail from cardboard (pattern page 151). Roll into conical shapes and tape to hold. Snip the wider ends of each cone and position against the body. Glue to hold.

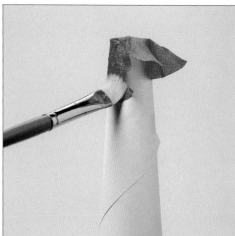

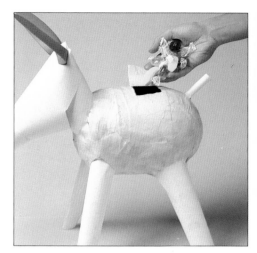

4 Cut the head and snout out of cardboard and attach to the neck with tape. Cut the ears, fold and staple. Attach to the head using double-sided tape.

5 Cut circles of crêpe paper to the correct sizes for the snout and socks. Clip the edges to 1¼ inches (3 cm) so that the pieces sit flat when glued to the body.

6 Cut a hole at the top of the body and remove the burst balloon. Fill the cavity with candy and re-close the opening with sticky tape.

7 Apply double-sided tape all over the *piñata*. Remove the protective strip in sections as you spiral the prepared frill (see page opposite) around the donkey.

8 For the saddle, wrap a band of crêpe paper around the girth and fasten with tape. Fasten bridle with eyelets using a riveter.

FINISHING THE PIÑATA

A bridle can be fashioned from brown cardboard cut into three ½ inch (1 cm) wide strips. Fasten them together with eyelets in the places indicated. Cut shapes for the eyes, draw pupils on them, and glue them to the head. To hang the *piñata*, tie a length of ribbon around the girth and another around the neck of the donkey. Attach a shorter strand between these two and tie a long ribbon onto it, tying the free end to a pole or tree branch.

MAKING PIÑATA FRILL

Crêpe paper, in two contrasting colors, is cut into strips, layered and then sewn and snipped to make the frill. Whether using each color separately or combining them for a variegated effect, several yards of frill will be needed to cover the *piñata*. The quantity used in this project was approximately 24½ feet (7.5 meters) of each color.

SEWING
Layer three strips of crêpe paper together and machine sew down the center along the full length of each strip.

FOLDING
Fold the sewn papers in half along the stitch line so that you have six paper layers.

SNIPPING
With scissors, snip the paper strip at ¼ inch (5 mm) intervals, being careful not to cut through the line of stitching. Ruffle the edges to separate the paper layers.

PROJECT: PAPEL PICADO PLACEMATS

For Mexicans, paper is not merely incidental to festivals and
ceremonies, it is a celebration in itself. The bright color and joyous
motifs of these papercut placemats are typical of Mexican design and
can bring a festive touch to any table.

Level of difficulty: Beginner

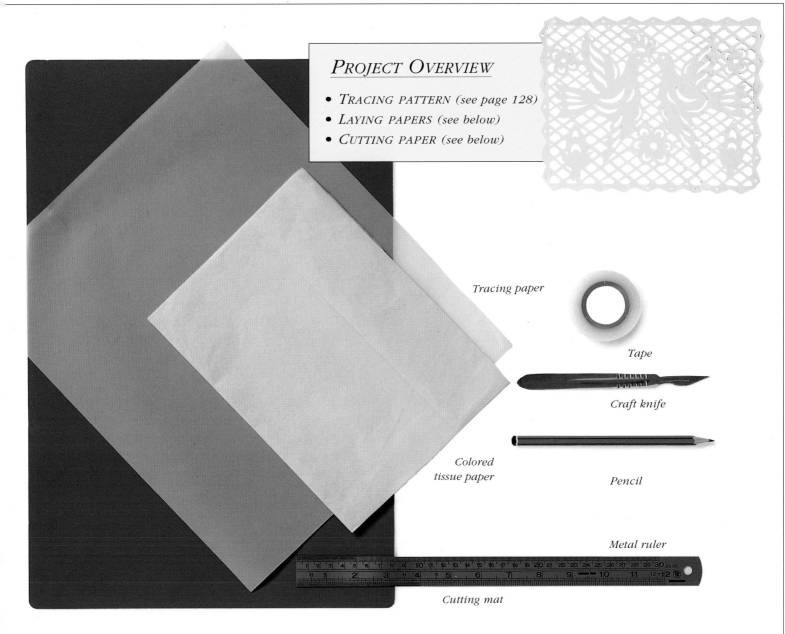

PROJECT OVERVIEW

- TRACING PATTERN (*see page 128*)
- LAYING PAPERS (*see below*)
- CUTTING PAPER (*see below*)

Tracing paper

Tape

Craft knife

Colored
tissue paper

Pencil

Metal ruler

Cutting mat

PLACEMATS STEP-BY-STEP

1 Lay four to six sheets of colored tissue paper on top of one another. Tape the stack at its four corners onto a cutting mat to secure before cutting.

2 Trace the design (pattern page 152) onto tracing paper and tape it over the stack of tissue paper. Cut the design with a craft knife, starting from the center.

3 Cut the serrated outside edges along a metal ruler using a craft knife. Cut all the diagonal lines in one direction first, then cut the others. Separate the placemats.

MARBLING

MARBLED PAPER is a record of moving water, its currents and eddies captured in graceful swirls of ink. The technique was called marbling because the earliest examples resembled the veined appearance of stone. Made by patterning colored pigments on liquid then lifting them off the surface with a sheet of paper, the resulting papers have been admired and sought after for centuries.

Marbled-edged books

Japanese legend asserts that the mysteries of marbling, or *suminagashi*, were divinely divulged to a mortal in 1151 as a reward for his piety. Historians prefer to argue, however, that the courtly Japanese game of submerging ink-painted pictures in water to 'release' the image may have prompted the notion of collecting the floating inks on paper. A more pragmatic theory suggests that marbling developed from the ancient practice of dyeing papers in colored insecticides. Whatever the origins of the technique, one thing is certain; for almost the whole length of its history, marbling remained an arcane craft and its secrets were jealously guarded.

Despite the vigilance of the Japanese royals, the technique of marbling began to work its way westward. Traveling along the silk trade routes, it was adopted and developed by many peoples. By the time it reached Turkey in the thirteenth century it had evolved into the sophisticated technique recognized in the West today. The subsequent spread of the craft through Europe occurred slowly but inevitably.

Marbling initially fulfilled a purely decorative need. Gifts of marbled papers were exchanged between nobles, and framed papers were frequently displayed on walls. But it was with the Renaissance - the golden age of book binding - that marbled papers ultimately came into their own. Bookbinders added marbling to their repertoire of skills, and particular designs came to be associated with individual workshops or the country of their origin. Some famous ones include Old Dutch, Morris and the French Curl.

The mid-nineteenth century saw the publication of the first manuals on the method of marbling. With these, marbling finally relinquished its mysteriousness and revealed its beautiful secrets to the world.

Marbled ornament

Marbling has traditionally been associated with the book-binding trade, but the papers can be used to decorate a range of items.

A traditional Turkish pattern

DESIGNS AND VARIATIONS

Two traditions encompass the craft of marbling, but within each of these can be discovered a wealth of styles and techniques. The type of marbling medium, the colors employed, the way the paints are manipulated: these factors, plus an incalculable number more, will determine the appearance of the finished sheet of paper.

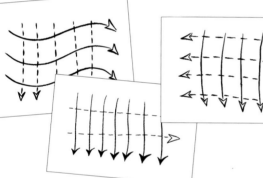

TURKISH MARBLING
Flowers are often represented by the Turkish style of marbling, popularized early this century.

MANIPULATING PATTERNS
Using a probe to tease droplets of color makes it possible to 'paint' images. The arrows shown on the illustrations to the left and right indicate the movements needed to complete each pattern.

OLD DUTCH

PEACOCK

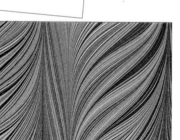

GET-GEL

FOUNTAIN

CHEVRON

TRADITIONAL PATTERNS
A number of popular marbling patterns are based on specific raking techniques. Many of the patterns shown here use a preliminary nonpareil base, made by raking from left to right then top to bottom in either a straight or a waved motion (see illustration above left).

COLOR
Used to make decorative objects like these lamp shades, marbled papers can reveal the full richness and depth of their hues.

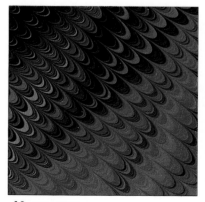

NONPAREIL

FLOWER DESIGNS

Dragging first inwards then outwards around the edge of a droplet of paint produces a daisy-like marbled image.

BIRD IN FLIGHT

Follow the direction of the arrows as indicated to create a flying bird.

BOOK BINDING

Marbled papers, traditionally used in book binding, give a professional finish to these ledgers.

BOUQUET

GOTHIC WAVE

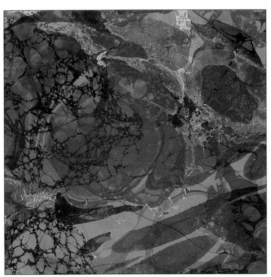

FLAME

FRENCH CURL

STONE (DOUBLE-PRINTED)

STATIONERY

One of the more favored uses for marbled papers is in the making of stationery.

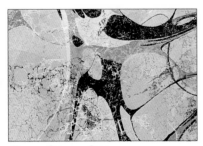

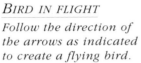

FREE STYLE STONE

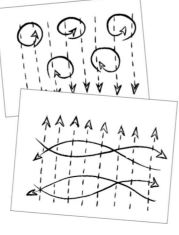

PROJECT: WATERCOLOR MARBLING

Watercolor marbling allows you considerable control in manipulating
paints on a sized water surface. The fluid, wavelike patterns of this
marbling design, properly called the bouquet design, are achieved
by a series of simple raking and combing motions.

Level of difficulty: Intermediate

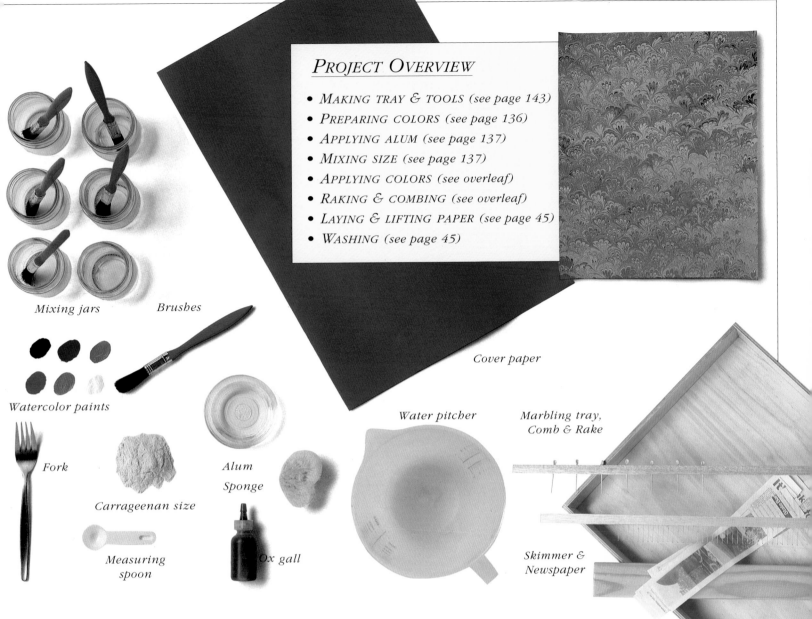

Mixing jars   Brushes

PROJECT OVERVIEW

- *MAKING TRAY & TOOLS (see page 143)*
- *PREPARING COLORS (see page 136)*
- *APPLYING ALUM (see page 137)*
- *MIXING SIZE (see page 137)*
- *APPLYING COLORS (see overleaf)*
- *RAKING & COMBING (see overleaf)*
- *LAYING & LIFTING PAPER (see page 45)*
- *WASHING (see page 45)*

Cover paper

Watercolor paints

Fork

Carrageenan size

Alum

Sponge

Water pitcher

Marbling tray,
Comb & Rake

Measuring
spoon

Ox gall

Skimmer &
Newspaper

MARBLING STEP-BY-STEP

1 Using a different jar for each color, mix four parts of water to one part of watercolor paint (see page 136). Add one drop of ox gall to each color and stir well with a fork. Test the colors (see page 136).

2 Apply alum to the paper (see page 137) and leave aside for at least 30 minutes. Mix the carrageenan marbling size (see page 137) and pour it into the tray. Skim the surface with the skimmer.

3 Cut strips of newspaper to a length 4 inches (10 cm) longer than the width of the tray. Skim the surface of the size mixture to eliminate dust, keeping the newspaper taut and skimming right to the edges of the tray.

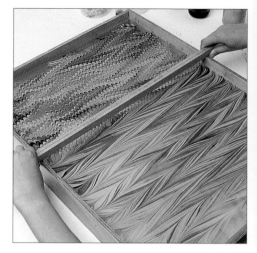

4 Apply the watercolor paints in the order in which they were tested, using a separate brush for each color. Gently tap droplets of each color onto the surface of the size.

5 From the top of the tray, smoothly drag the rake towards you to the bottom. Without lifting the rake, center the prongs between the tracks of the rake's previous pass and return it to the top.

6 Rake from the right to the left side of the tray and then back again. Then insert the comb at the top of the tray and drag it down once. Finally, rake twice in a zigzag motion from the top (see below).

RAKING & COMBING

The final raking motion which completes the bouquet pattern is achieved by positioning the rake in the size mixture at the end of the tray and slowly pulling the rake towards you in a zigzag motion. Each inflection should be about 2 inches (5 cm) long. Lift the rake out of the tray and position it at the top so that the prongs lie in between the previous rake tracks. Repeat the zigzag motion, pulling in the opposite direction (see diagram on page opposite).

7 With the alum-coated side of the paper facing down, lower one corner onto the surface of the liquid, then lay the whole sheet down in a smooth rolling motion, allowing any trapped air to escape.

8 Insert the wash board into the tray and rub a little of the size onto the board, using your fingers. Lift the paper out of the water and lay it against the board, pattern side facing outwards.

9 Ladle clean water over the print to wash off the size. Wash the back too, folding the sheet over itself lengthways one way and then the other and rinsing each time. Hang the sheet up to dry.

MARBLING STAGES

Use the swatches below as a guide to how the surface of your tray should look at each of the raking and combing stages. But remember, it is impossible to replicate a marbled design exactly.

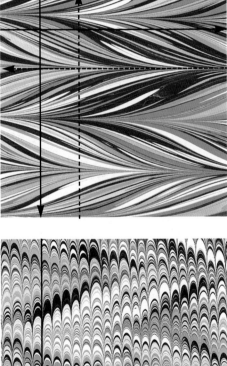

2. Pass the rake smoothly from the top to the bottom of the tray. Shift 1 inch (2.5 cm) to the left and drag the rake back to the top of the tray. Then insert the rake along the left side of the tray and pass it from left to right and back again.

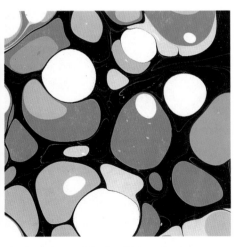

1. Starting with the first color you tested, apply droplets of paint over the entire tray. Gently tap each of the loaded brushes against your other hand to release the paint.

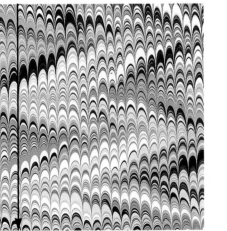

3. Insert the comb at the top of the tray and drag it to the bottom using a smooth, quick pulling motion.

4. Use the rake to zigzag downwards from the top of the tray. Re-position it at the top so that it bisects the tracks of the previous pass and zigzag down again, crossing your previous zigzag.

PROJECT: TURKISH MARBLING

The style of marbling commonly known as Turkish was developed at the beginning of this century by Necmeddin Okyay, whose speciality was the drawing of realistic flowers on a marbling size. This project captures on paper the beauty and individuality of the technique he popularized.

Level of difficulty: Advanced

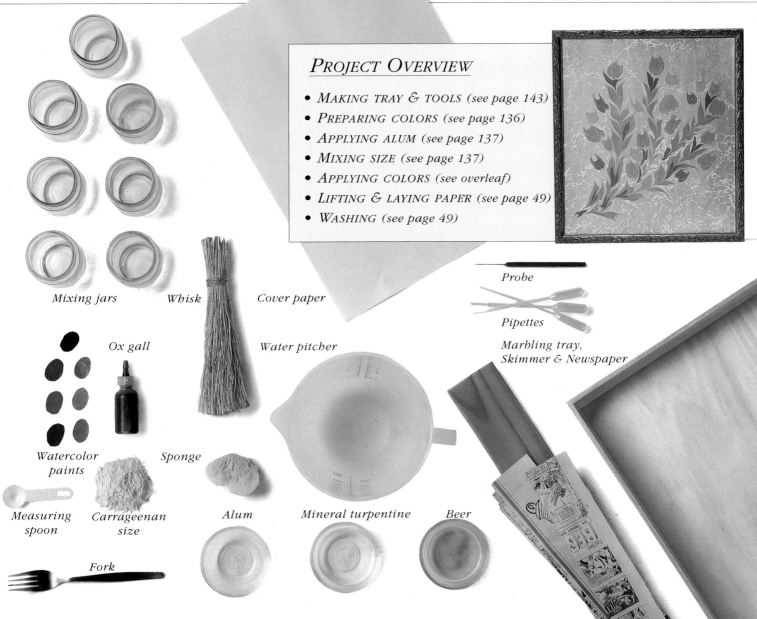

PROJECT OVERVIEW

- MAKING TRAY & TOOLS (see page 143)
- PREPARING COLORS (see page 136)
- APPLYING ALUM (see page 137)
- MIXING SIZE (see page 137)
- APPLYING COLORS (see overleaf)
- LIFTING & LAYING PAPER (see page 49)
- WASHING (see page 49)

Mixing jars   Whisk   Cover paper

Probe

Pipettes

Marbling tray,
Skimmer & Newspaper

Ox gall

Water pitcher

Watercolor
paints   Sponge

Measuring
spoon

Carrageenan
size

Alum

Mineral turpentine

Beer

Fork

TURKISH MARBLING STEP-BY-STEP

1 Mix the watercolor paints (see page 136), adding ox gall to all colors except the background indigo. To this add four drops of turpentine and one teaspoon of beer to give it an oily, bubbly texture.

2 Apply alum to the paper and leave aside for at least 30 minutes. Make the carageenan size (see page 137) and pour into the tray. Drag the skimmer down the tray to rid the surface of dust or air bubbles.

3 Skim the surface again, this time with strips of newspaper. It is important to skim to the edges of the tray. Dip the whisk into the indigo paint, shaking excess into the jar, and splatter over the size (see overleaf).

4 To apply the green paint for the leaves, use a pipette to deposit two or three droplets of paint for each leaf onto the surface. Arrange the colors according to the photograph on the previous page.

5 Use the probe to make the leaves. First, drag down through the center of the dots to make heart shapes, then up through the two mounds of each heart to make the points (see facing page).

6 Apply the remaining colors for the flowers. Use the probe to make petal shapes resembling tulips. Do this by dragging the outer edges of each dot upwards (see facing page).

APPLYING PAINT WITH A WHISK

Whisks, made from millet straw, hold a limited amount of paint. To encourage the paint to fall evenly over the surface of the size mixture, gently but firmly tap the whisk against your other hand or, if you prefer, against a stick. See page 145 for instructions on how to make a whisk.

STAGES FOR CREATING TULIPS

The guide below shows you how to make one stem. Make all the stems at the same time, performing each step on every stem before proceeding to the next step. The tools required to produce the design are a pipette and a probe.

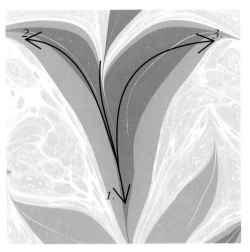

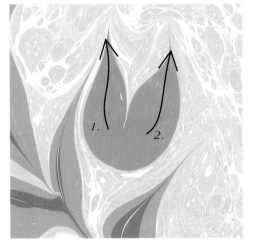

2. Drag the dots with the probe to shape the leaves, pulling in the directions indicated by the arrows.

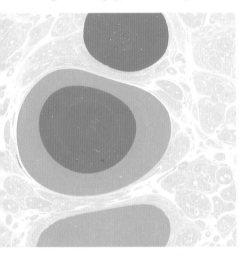

1. Using a pipette, dot the surface of the size mixture with the paler shade of green, then apply the darker shade of green on top of the light spots.

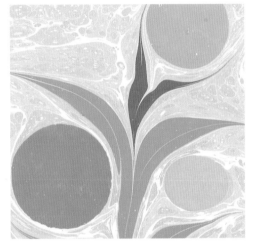

3. Apply the pink, mauve and pale blue colors for the flowers with a pipette.

4. Shape the flowers by dragging the dots in the directions indicated by the arrows.

7 With the alum-coated side facing down, lower one corner of the sheet of paper onto the surface of the liquid. Then lay the whole sheet down in a rolling motion, allowing any trapped air to escape.

8 Insert the wash board into the tray and rub a little of the size mixture from the tray onto the board. Lift the paper out of the water and lay it against the board, pattern side facing outwards.

9 Ladle clean water over the paper to wash off the size. Wash the back as well as the front to prevent the sheet from warping when dry. Allow the water to run off before hanging the sheet up to dry.

PROJECT: OIL MARBLED COMPENDIUM

Oil color marbling is the oldest form of paper marbling and its veined, stone-like images bear an appropriately ancient appearance. Create patterned paper of fascinating beauty using gold and black oil paint on a rich red background, and use it to cover a compendium for holding stationery.

Level of difficulty: Beginner

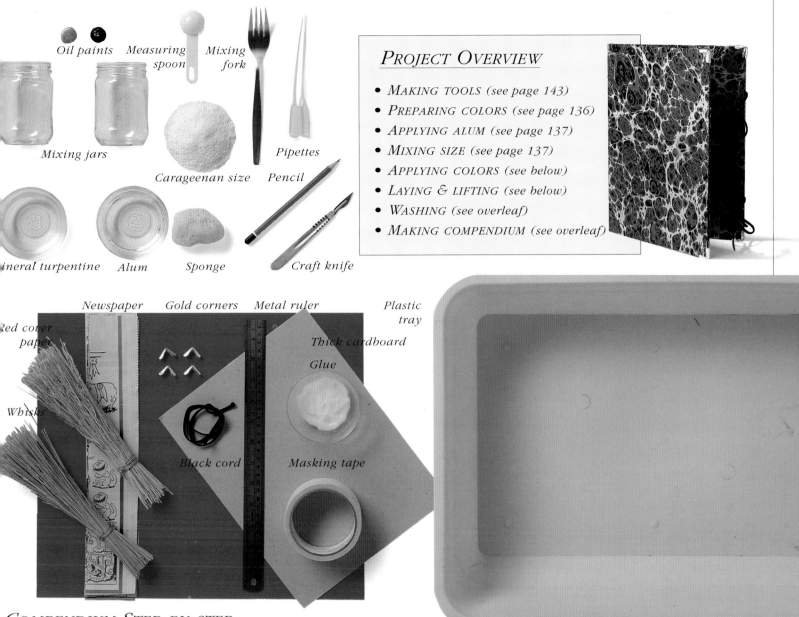

Oil paints Measuring Mixing
spoon   fork

Mixing jars

Carageenan size Pencil

Pipettes

ineral turpentine Alum Sponge

Craft knife

PROJECT OVERVIEW

- *MAKING TOOLS (see page 143)*
- *PREPARING COLORS (see page 136)*
- *APPLYING ALUM (see page 137)*
- *MIXING SIZE (see page 137)*
- *APPLYING COLORS (see below)*
- *LAYING & LIFTING (see below)*
- *WASHING (see overleaf)*
- *MAKING COMPENDIUM (see overleaf)*

Red cover
paper

Newspaper Gold corners Metal ruler

Plastic
tray

Thick cardboard

Glue

Whisks

Black cord Masking tape

COMPENDIUM STEP-BY-STEP

1 Apply alum to the sheet of red cover paper and set aside for 30 minutes. Into the tray pour the prepared carrageenan size (see page 137). Prepare and test the oil colors (see page 136).

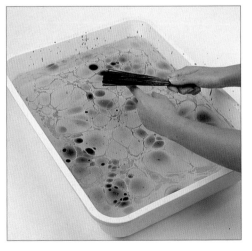

2 Dip the whisk into the prepared gold paint and splatter onto the surface of the water by tapping the whisk against your other hand. Using a clean whisk, apply black paint over the gold in the same way.

3 With the alum-coated side facing down, lower one corner of the sheet of paper onto the surface of the liquid. Then lay the whole sheet down in a smooth rolling motion to expel any air bubbles.

  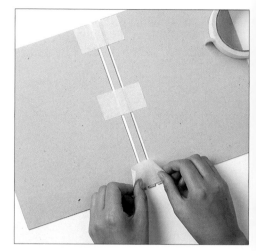

4 Gently lift the marbled paper off the tray and wash off the size by holding the marbled print over a bucket and ladling clean water over the sheet, rinsing both the back and front. Allow most of the water to run off before hanging the sheet up to dry.

5 On cardboard, draw two large rectangles, 10 x 7 inches (25 x 18 cm), and two narrow rectangles, 10 x 3 inches (25 x 8 cm). Draw a strip, 10 x ½ inches (25 cm x 10 mm). Measure the pieces accurately and cut out with a craft knife against a metal ruler.

6 Position the ½ inch (10 mm) strip of cardboard between the two large rectangles as shown, leaving a gap between each piece which is twice as wide as the thickness of the cardboard. Apply strips of tape in three places to join the pieces.

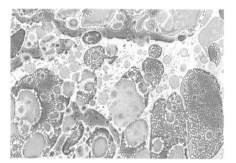

Violet, blue, yellow and green printed once on a white background.

OTHER EFFECTS WITH OIL MARBLING

By overprinting, by using different colored papers and by manipulating paints on the size surface, a variety of oil marbling effects can be achieved. Unlike watercolor marbling, which permits the application of a large number of paints at once, the oil paint technique is intolerant of too many colours being laid (three or four is usual). But even with a limited palette, beautiful and diverse effects can be achieved. In the swatches below the same colors have been used each time, but, by using different colored paper, and by overprinting, a diverse range of effects have been created.

The same colors overprinted on green paper. Marbling on colored paper intensifies the hues.

Overprinting onto orange paper brings depth and richness to the colors.

When marbling on blue paper, a small amount of blue is effectively added to every pigment used.

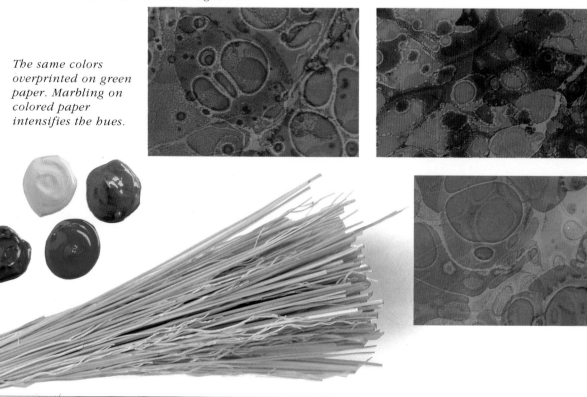

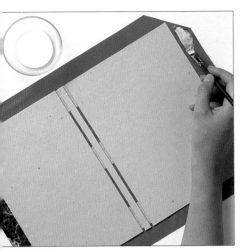

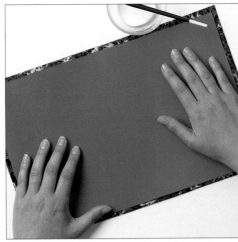

7 Cut a 11½ x 16 inch (29 x 41 cm) rectangle from the marbled paper. Brush glue onto the back of the hinged cardboard, center over the marbled paper and press in place. Trim the corners and glue down the flaps. Fold flaps to the inside.

8 Cut a 14 x 9½ inch (36 x 24 cm) rectangle from the plain red paper. Apply a thin coat of glue over the back of the paper, center it over the inside of the compendium and press in place. Crease the paper where it folds into the hinges.

9 Cut two pieces, 10⅔ x 4 inches (27 x 10 cm), from the marbled paper for covering the inner sleeves. Attach with glue, trim the edges, then glue flaps to the inside. Glue cords between the covers and sleeves, glue the sleeves in place (see below).

FINISHING THE COMPENDIUM

Cut four lengths of black cord, 10 inches (25 cm) each. Dip the ends of each into glue to prevent them from fraying. Measure and mark on the inside of each vertical side of the compendium two points, each 2½ inches (6 cm) down from the corners. Apply glue to these four points and press the lengths of cord in place so that the tail of each lies away from the compendium. Apply a line of glue around three sides of the sleeves and press each in place on the inside covers of the compendium so that the unglued edge is innermost. Hold firmly until dry. Finish the compendium with gold metallic corners.

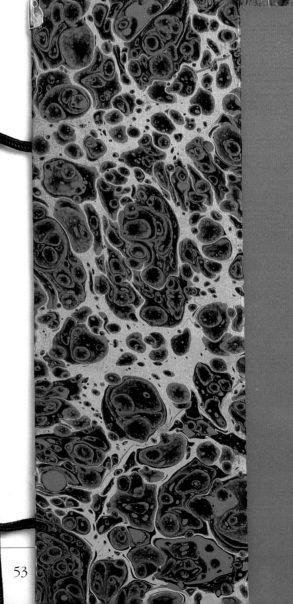

DÉCOUPAGE

DÉCOUPAGE, with its sepia-hued flowers and foliage, graceful wreaths and garlands, madonnas and cupids, is the art of deception. Created by layering many coats of varnish over an arrangement of cut-out paper images, découpage draws us into a world of fantasy, denying its humble materials with its counterfeit paintwork and enthralling us with its beauty.

English plates from 1890

The word découpage is derived from the French word *couper*, meaning 'to cut,' but the discovery of the craft can be attributed to the Chinese, who were decorating objects with silk cuttings at least as early as the fifteenth century. It was in the seventeenth century in Italy, however, that paper découpage achieved widespread popularity. Painted and gilded furniture was much in demand at this time, and it was in response to the costliness of the genuine article that people began cutting up prints and encasing them under layers of varnish. Scornfully dubbed *l'arte del povero*, 'the poor man's art,' découpage soon became a fashionable creative pursuit for gentlefolk.

At the French court of Louis XVI, Marie Antoinette and her courtiers were notorious for cutting up original paintings and applying them to fans, boxes and screens. The terrible cost of this activity, both to the purse and to the art world, was eliminated in the next wave of découpage enthusiasm, which occurred with the advent of color printing. The quantity of good quality printed material that became available in the mid nineteenth century encouraged the Victorians to adopt the craft en masse. Paper images were cut from everything from catalogues to cards and were avidly collected and swapped. By the end of the century, special sheets of découpage images, or 'scraps,' were even being printed.

Edwardian scrap book

Today the term découpage can be applied to as many different styles as the papers can be applied to objects. From the ebullience of the baroque and the delicacy of the rococo to the romanticism of the Victorians and the liberalism of the modern age, découpage has proved its great versatility and abiding popularity.

Découpage can be applied to a range of objects.

Découpage tray in the rococo style

DESIGNS AND VARIATIONS

While the technique of decorating objects with paper cut-outs has remained largely unchanged for the whole of its history, the range of découpage styles has shown no such steadfastness. Découpage has been categorized under such descriptive titles as *grotesque*, *Chinoiserie*, *milles fleurs* and *trompe l'oeil*, but the craft has ultimately proved itself an indefinable one. Sometimes called the chameleon of papercrafts, the huge range of styles justifies the description.

HAT BOX
Religious imagery is commonly found in old découpage pieces.

THE LAYERING OF IMAGES AND VARNISH

Layers of varnish
Paper images

Background image

Object surface

IMAGE COLLECTING

In Victorian times, when découpage was at the height of its popularity, pre-cut images were sold. Contemporary découpeurs use books, magazines, wrapping papers, greetings cards and drawings as image sources.

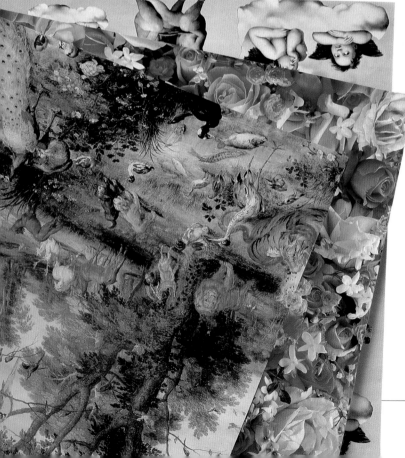

CRAZY QUILT STYLE
Large and small prints are combined so that no single image or color dominates, as on this card table.

ILLUMINATED ANGEL

Foil can be used as a device to create highlights. This classical image is given brilliance with highlights of gold foil.

FOIL HIGHLIGHTS

Lay down a sheet of foil, then cut slits in the uppermost image with a craft knife to create highlights.

CARDS

Old postcards and greeting cards can impart an aged, nostalgic look. Thin them first by soaking in water then peeling off the cardboard backing.

MODERN PLATES

Découpage traditionally uses subdued colors, but the bright colors of these contemporary plates are just as effective.

THREE-DIMENSIONAL DÉCOUPAGE

To give an image depth, use a pin to prick a spiral over the design element. Turn the image over and gently rub the paper to stretch it into a concave shape. Fill the hollow with glue, then turn it over and glue in place.

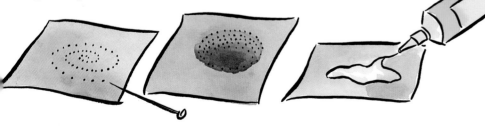

PROJECT: DÉCOUPAGE BOOK BOX

Luxuriant images and warm glowing colors give this book box a
sumptuousness which layers upon layers of varnish enhance to
wonderful effect. The paper cuttings used here are selected from early
nineteenth century reprints of oil paintings and botanical illustrations.

Level of difficulty: Beginner

PROJECT OVERVIEW

- SEALING *(see page 139)*
- CUTTING IMAGES *(see overleaf)*
- ARRANGING IMAGES *(see overleaf)*
- GLUING IMAGES *(see below)*
- SANDING *(see page 138)*
- VARNISHING *(see page 139)*

Color images

Sandpaper & Sanding block

Removable adhesive

Cuticle scissors

Varnish & Flat brush

Sealer

Sponge brush

Water-based glue

Roller

Colored pencils

Lint-free cloth & Tack cloth

BOOK BOX STEP-BY-STEP

1 Coat all the outer surfaces of the book box with sealer. Cut from paper two background images for the front and back and coat both sides of the images with the sealer. Allow the surfaces to dry.

2 Apply glue to the front of the box and position the background image. Smear more glue on top and roll lightly from the center to the edges, pushing out any excess glue. Do the same for the back.

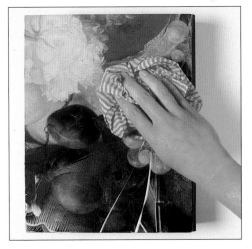

3 Wipe off any remaining glue with a damp cloth. Carefully massage any air bubbles or pockets of excess glue to the nearest edge, dipping your fingertips in water first to lubricate the surface.

4 After cutting out each image (see below), place them in an aesthetically pleasing arrangement. Re-usable adhesive is helpful in positioning your design; remove it before you glue each image down.

5 Starting with the images in the background areas, glue all the paper cut-outs to the lid. For best results, allow each piece to dry a little before applying the next. Allow the whole piece to dry.

6 Color any white paper showing around the edges of the images with colored pencils so that the images blend into the background. Good quality wax- or oil-based pencils are best for this purpose.

CUTTING OUT A DÉCOUPAGE IMAGE

When cutting, keep your scissor hand steady and move the paper with your other hand. Whether using cuticle scissors or a razor, make your cuts so that they slant away from the image. This is called beveling and is done to avoid white edges showing when the images are glued down. Do not be afraid to cut your paper images inside their printed borders; bold and imaginative re-shaping makes for a more interesting piece.

7 Apply two coats of sealer to the box, painting in opposite directions with each application. This will prevent the finishing coats from bleeding or bruising into the raw edges of the images.

8 Apply enough coats of varnish to build up a thick finish. Oil-based varnishes require 20-30 coats; water-based varnishes need even more. Allow time for the varnish to dry between coats.

9 When the images are well encased in varnish, start sanding between coats using 280 grade wet-and-dry sandpaper. Use progressively finer sand-papers and wipe with a tack cloth after sanding.

DIFFERENT DÉCOUPAGE FINISHES

VARNISHES
Water-based and oil-based varnishes require many coats. Apply the varnish with a good brush, allowing it to dry completely before applying the next coat.

RESIN
A quick alternative to varnish is resin, a one-coat finish. The two parts of the resin coating are mixed together then applied with a paint brush. Drinking straws and a flame torch are used to dissipate air bubbles.

WAX
For a simple, sweet-smelling wax finish, rub the découpage surface with fine steel wool then apply beeswax in circular motions with the steel wool. When the wax is dry, buff the surface with a soft cloth.

ANTIQUING
To simulate aging, rub a small amount of patina onto an object, then apply brown oil paint on a rag. Wipe with a lint-free cloth to remove most of the paint.

PROJECT: DÉCOUPAGE VASE

With its free, asymmetrical forms, its lightness and delicacy, this vase is a modern interpretation of the traditional rococo style of découpage. The design features classical cupid and flower motifs placed against a sapphire and gold sponged background.

Level of difficulty: Intermediate

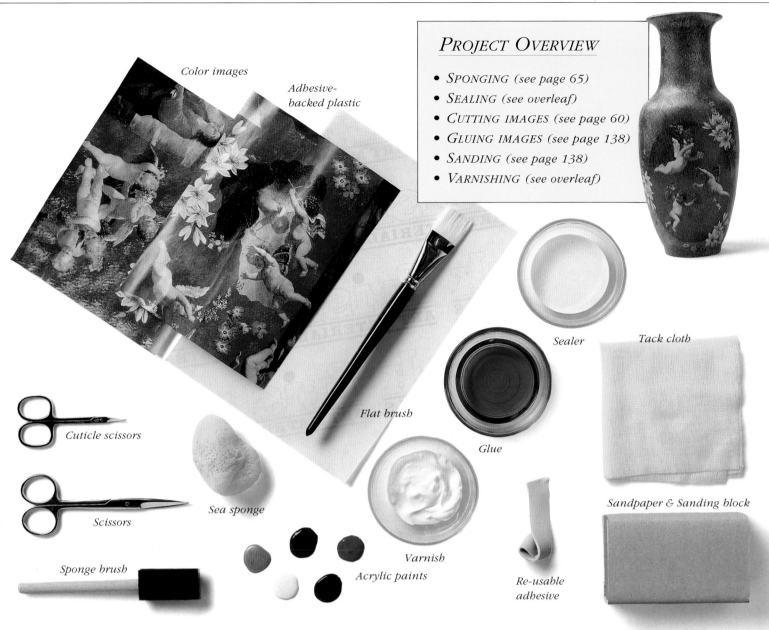

Color images

Adhesive-
backed plastic

PROJECT OVERVIEW

- SPONGING (see page 65)
- SEALING (see overleaf)
- CUTTING IMAGES (see page 60)
- GLUING IMAGES (see page 138)
- SANDING (see page 138)
- VARNISHING (see overleaf)

Sealer

Tack cloth

Flat brush

Glue

Cuticle scissors

Scissors

Sea sponge

Sandpaper & Sanding block

Sponge brush

Varnish

Acrylic paints

Re-usable
adhesive

VASE STEP-BY-STEP

1 Basecoat the bisque vase with dark brown acrylic paint. From adhesive-backed plastic cut an oval mask to suit the size of the vase and apply it to the vase.

2 Using the sea sponge, lightly apply each of the four remaining colors onto the vase. Follow the sponging instructions on page 65. Allow to dry.

3 Carefully remove the mask from the vase and sponge gold paint over the exposed area of the oval. Thin with water if necessary. Allow the paint to fully dry.

4 Sponge a coat of blue paint on the oval area. Sponge slightly over the edge of the oval to make the paint blend with the background colors. Allow to dry.

5 Use a clean sponge brush to apply a smooth coat of sealer over the entire surface of the vase, sealing as far inside the neck as possible. Allow the sealer to dry.

6 Cut out the images and leave them unsealed (see page 139). With re-usable adhesive, arrange the images on the vase. Glue, removing adhesive as you go.

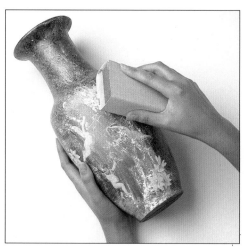

7 When the glue has dried completely, apply an even coat of varnish to the vase. Paint with many coats of varnish, allowing time to dry between each one.

8 Lightly sand the vase, remove the dust and grit with a tack cloth and apply another coat of varnish. For other découpage finishes see page 61.

GLUING THE IMAGES

Rub a generous amount of glue onto the area where the image is to be adhered. Position the image and gently apply more glue over it, expelling any air bubbles or extra glue with your fingers. Wipe a soft, damp cloth over the surface to remove the excess glue.

SPONGING STAGES

1. Sponge blue paint over the brown basecoat.

2. Lightly apply white paint on top of the blue.

3. Sponge again with blue paint.

4. Apply gold paint with the sponge brush.

5. Finish sponging with rust-red paint.

JAPANESE PAPERCRAFT

CARP STREAMERS *swimming brightly in the wind, paper dolls in flowing white kimonos, gauzelike paper lanterns and intricate origami figures are all frequent images of Japanese life. In a society dominated by rationalism and efficiency, papercrafts are made with painstaking care, a testament to the regard with which the Japanese hold the beautiful medium of paper.*

Festivals, rituals, social occasions, food and dress all utilize paper in its various manifestations.

Hexagonal origami box   Ricepaper, originally brought to the Japanese archipelago by Chinese Buddhist priests almost two thousand years ago, combines thinness and pliancy with great tensile strength. Lanterns, umbrellas, screens and fans translucently reveal the fine qualities of this material.

A notable use of paper is in the making of dolls. One variety is the *shiso ningyo*, molded with a pasty mixture of rice paper fibers and wheat starch. A variation of this doll is the *washibari ningyo*, which is made by pasting tiny pieces of Japanese paper onto the molded body of a doll.

Shibusa, or 'tastefulness,' is the Japanese concept of beauty.

It includes ideas of simplicity, quietude and propriety which are captured in the beautiful *washi chigiri-e* creations of its artists. Literally meaning 'torn rice paper,' *washi chigiri-e* uses thumbnail-sized pieces of colored paper to make decorative pictures, often of flowers and landscapes.

But the Japanese sense of understatement is perhaps best accomplished in paper with the craft of *origami.* An art of suggestion, *origami* implies without announcing outright. Folding paper is an exercise in mathematics as much as in art.

In a country where   *Samurai-inspired paper doll*
no gift is given unwrapped, no wedding celebrated without the blessing of paper butterflies and no shrine decorated without a row of paper lanterns, the significance of this ephemeral material to Japanese society cannot be underestimated. Japanese papercrafts have the capacity to dignify whatever or whoever they touch with their unique beauty.

Strings of multicolored origami cranes

Paper pervades every arena of Japanese life; a fan-bearing woman stands before a paper screen wearing ornaments of paper in her hair.

DESIGNS AND VARIATIONS

Japanese papercrafts are a dedication to the aesthetic qualities of their medium. The functionality of a paper creation is often considered secondary to the beauty of the finished object. Origami and doll-making, two of Japan's most popular papercrafts, are supreme examples of this love of paper for its own sake. But even when serving practical needs, Japanese papercrafts are never lacking in beauty or style.

PAPER LANTERN
A Japanese lantern is painted with a delicate floral design.

FANS
Born of the need to keep cool in summer, paper fans become beautiful creations in the hands of their Japanese makers.

GIRLS' DAY
Paper dolls called hina ningyo *are the centerpiece of an annual celebration of and for girls.*

ORIGAMI BOXES
Boxes are one of the most popular origami folds. The standard box fold can be translated into different forms with the use of traditional and modern papers.

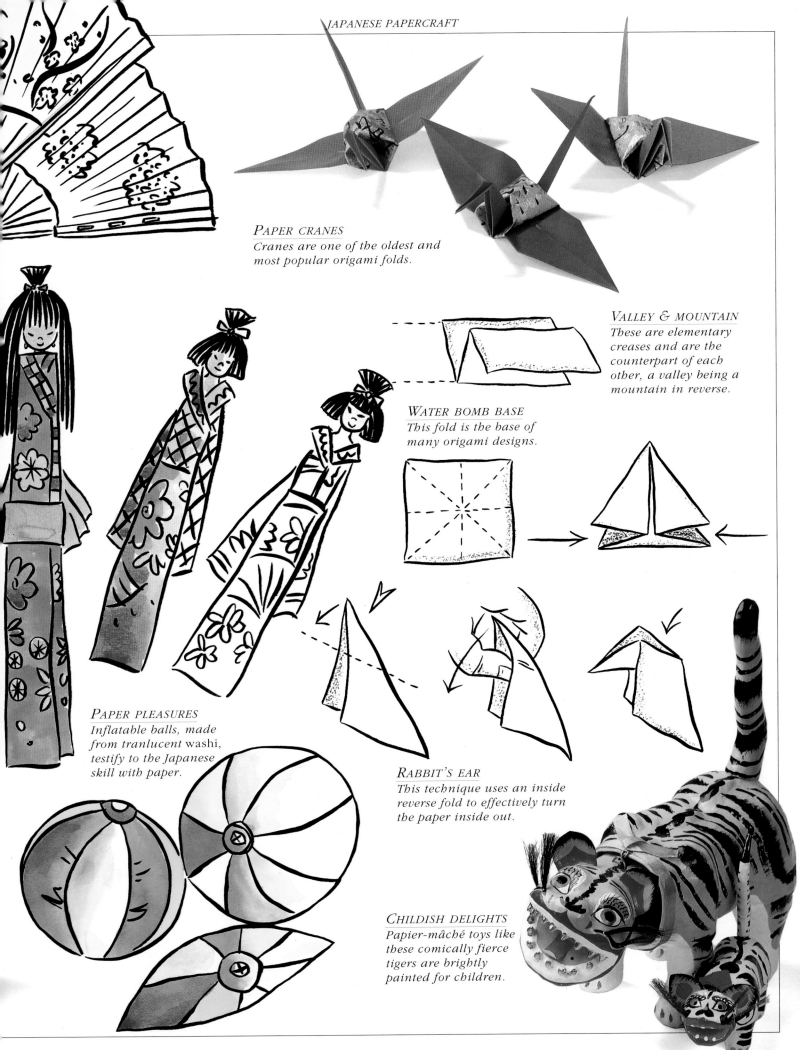

PAPER CRANES
Cranes are one of the oldest and most popular origami folds.

VALLEY & MOUNTAIN
These are elementary creases and are the counterpart of each other, a valley being a mountain in reverse.

WATER BOMB BASE
This fold is the base of many origami designs.

PAPER PLEASURES
Inflatable balls, made from tranlucent washi, testify to the Japanese skill with paper.

RABBIT'S EAR
This technique uses an inside reverse fold to effectively turn the paper inside out.

CHILDISH DELIGHTS
Papier-mâché toys like these comically fierce tigers are brightly painted for children.

PROJECT: SHIMADA *DOLL*

Shimada refers to a hairstyle which became popular among courtiers in the city of Shimada during the Ido period in the late eighteenth century. This elegant paper doll encapsulates the Japanese ideals of restraint and dignity.

Level of difficulty: Advanced

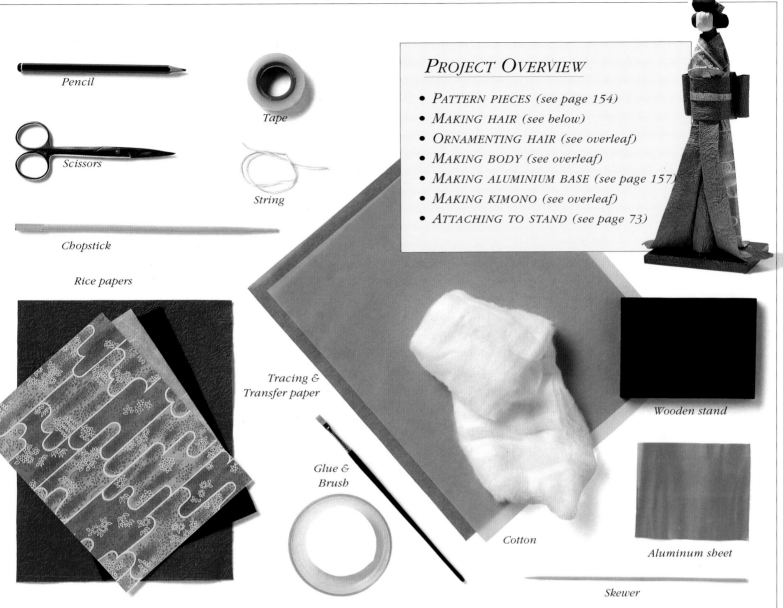

Pencil

Tape

Scissors

String

Chopstick

Rice papers

Tracing &
Transfer paper

Glue &
Brush

Cotton

Wooden stand

Aluminum sheet

Skewer

PROJECT OVERVIEW

- PATTERN PIECES (see page 154)
- MAKING HAIR (see below)
- ORNAMENTING HAIR (see overleaf)
- MAKING BODY (see overleaf)
- MAKING ALUMINIUM BASE (see page 157)
- MAKING KIMONO (see overleaf)
- ATTACHING TO STAND (see page 73)

SHIMADA DOLL STEP-BY-STEP

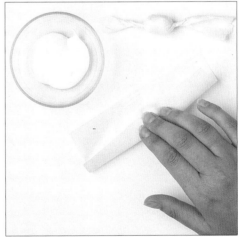

1 Following the patterns, trace and cut the hair pieces. Coil the main hair piece around a chopstick, leaving 4 inches (10 cm) unrolled. Remove the chopstick and insert a length of string through the coil.

2 Bring the ends of the coil around to meet each other by pulling the string, and tie a knot to hold the hair roll in place. The tail of the roll will later be inserted into the kimono to form the neck of the doll.

3 Cut a piece of white paper for the face according to pattern and place a ball of cotton in the center of it. Roll the paper lengthways and secure with glue, then twist the ends as if wrapping a bon-bon.

4 Insert one of the twisted tails into the main hair coil, bringing both tails together at the opening. Tie with string.

5 Fold the front hair piece according to the pattern. Gather, then tie the ends. Insert into the main hair piece and glue.

6 Fold the bun piece as indicated in the pattern. Fold around cotton and tie. Cut one tail in half, to the string.

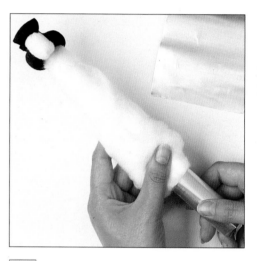

7 Twist the two strips just made by cutting the one tail in half. Tie them together in a knot as shown. Glue to hold.

8 Insert the bun into the center of the main hair piece, behind the front roll, the knotted ends forwards. Glue in place.

9 Push a skewer into the neck, glue and wrap in cotton. Wrap with aluminum (see page 157) and tape to body.

Attach the bow, comb and hair pin to the head with invisible dots of glue.

10 Cut strips of white paper according to the pattern. Coil tightly around the body from the neck down. Tape to hold.

11 Cut the collar and under-kimono pieces. Glue the collar around the neck and the kimono around the base.

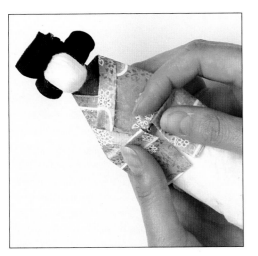

12 Cut the upper kimono piece and fold according to pattern. Wrap kimono around body, folding as shown, and glue.

13 Cut the plain and patterned pieces for the lower kimono and glue together. Wrap around the body, gluing in place.

14 Crease the lower back of the kimono at the sides and fold the kimono backwards and upwards to make a train.

15 Cut pieces for the obi bow and fold as indicated. Pinch the bow to gather before gluing. Loop and glue shorter strip.

16 Cut the wrap piece for the obi. Fold in edges as indicated. Wrap around the body, overlapping at the back, and glue.

To display the doll, glue the aluminum base of the doll to a black painted board. Hold in position until the glue is dry.

17 Cut sash piece for obi and fold edges in. Place around the wrap, passing it through the loop of the obi bow and gluing.

18 Cut the hair ornament pieces. Tie a flat knot for bow, cut comb and hat pin. Roll a tiny ball of paper for pin head.

PROJECT: ORIGAMI BOX

Paper wrappings become supremely beautiful creations in the hands
of Japanese craftspeople, and this origami box is no exception.
Made by pleating and folding squares of textured and patterned rice
papers, it is based on the traditional measuring box.

Level of difficulty: Beginner

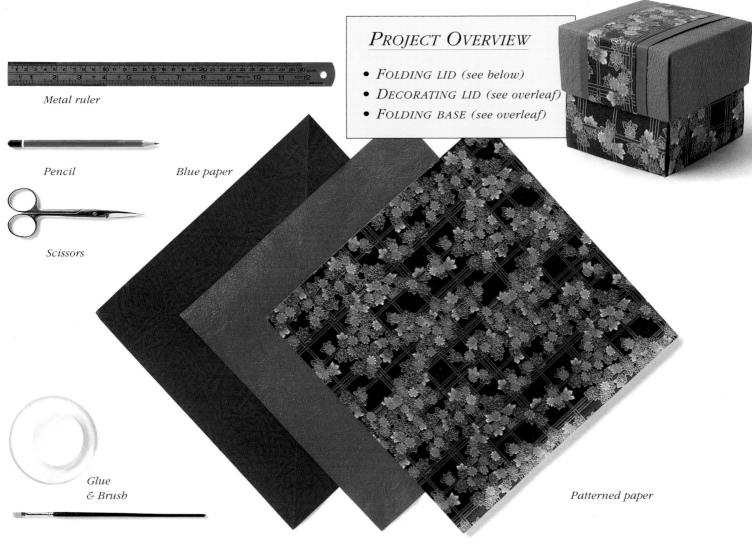

Metal ruler

Pencil

Blue paper

Scissors

PROJECT OVERVIEW

- *FOLDING LID (see below)*
- *DECORATING LID (see overleaf)*
- *FOLDING BASE (see overleaf)*

Glue
& Brush

Patterned paper

Red paper

BOX LID STEP-BY-STEP

1 Cut two squares of rice paper (pattern page 160). Glue together, crease along the marked lines and open out. Fold opposite corners to the center, then fold both over again to meet the central fold.

2 Bring the two edges you have just folded upwards to a vertical position to create the first two sides of the lid. The pointed flaps are folded and pressed flat against the inside base of the box.

3 Make the third side of the lid by pressing inwards at the diagonal pleat marks and folding the paper to make two troughs. This pulls the side up to vertical. Complete the fourth side in same way.

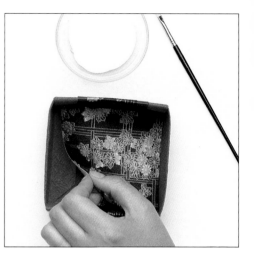

4 Fold the two protruding flaps over to the inside of the box to complete the lid. The points should lie flat against the inside base, next to those previously folded.

5 Make the decorative band (see below) and with the pattern side upwards, glue to the lid, starting at the inside base and wrapping it around to the other side.

6 Cut a 4 x 4 inch (10.5 x 10.5 cm) reinforcing square from the decorative paper. Glue to the inside base of the lid so that it covers the ends of the band.

CONSTRUCTING THE LID

To make the decorative band, cut two 15¾ x 4 inch (40 x 10 cm) strips from each of the blue and patterned papers. Fold the long sides of the strips underneath to hide the cut edges, the blue to a width of 2½ inches (6.5 cm) and the patterned to 2 inches (5 cm). Glue the bands with their folded sides facing so that the patterned band is positioned along the center of the plain band.

The pleat marks are pressed in to push the paper into troughs, forcing the sides of the lid upwards to the vertical position.

A square of patterned paper fits the inside of the lid, reinforcing it as well as serving a decorative function.

The band is wrapped around the lid prior to adhering the reinforcing square in place.

The first and second sides of the box are simply made by double-folding the corners.

BOX BASE STEP-BY-STEP

1 Cut two squares of paper (pattern page 159) and glue together. Crease along the marked lines, unfold. Fold diagonally, then fold the two points inwards.

2 Open these two points and squash each fold by inserting fingers between the two layers and pushing the spine to meet the edge of the flattened crease mark.

3 Unfold the sheet, turn 90° and repeat the folds of steps 1 and 2; unfold. Bring the two outer creases of one corner together, folding the excess paper inwards.

4 Without letting go of the edges you have just brought together, bring the inside flap forward so that it lies flat against two sides of the box, reinforcing the corner.

5 Secure the corner by folding the small, protruding triangle forward over the lip of the box and make a sharp crease, then pinch to make the vertical crease.

6 Complete each of the remaining three corners of the box in the same way, making sure that all of the creases are crisp and straight. Put the lid on the finished box.

PROJECT: WASHI CHIGIRI-E

Tearing small pieces of colored rice paper and arranging them into pictures is a Japanese art dating back almost two thousand years. As old as paper itself, the survival of the art of *washi chigiri-e* is a sign of the continuing popularity of this simple yet beautiful paper craft.

Level of difficulty: Beginner

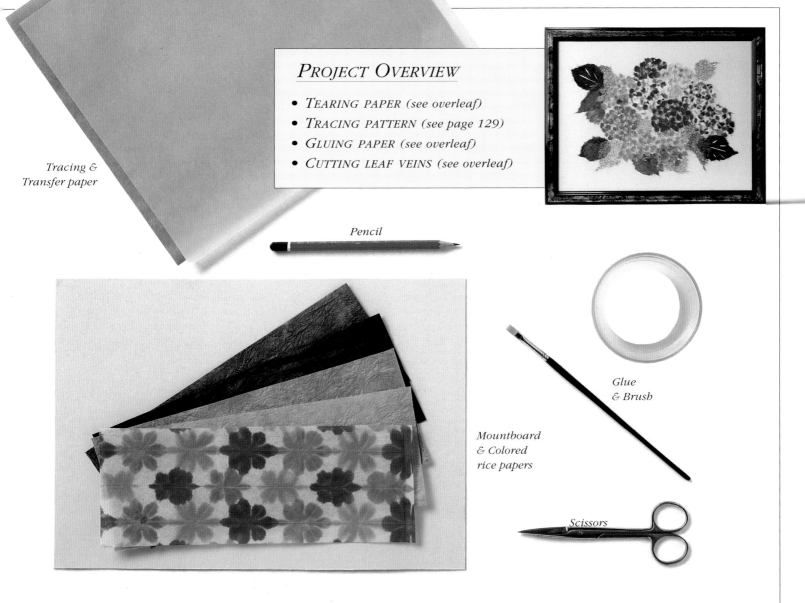

PROJECT OVERVIEW

- *TEARING PAPER* (see overleaf)
- *TRACING PATTERN* (see page 129)
- *GLUING PAPER* (see overleaf)
- *CUTTING LEAF VEINS* (see overleaf)

*Tracing &
Transfer paper*

Pencil

*Glue
& Brush*

*Mountboard
& Colored
rice papers*

Scissors

WASHI CHIGIRI-E *STEP-BY-STEP*

1 Reserving most of the green paper for making the leaves at step 5, tear the colored rice paper into small circles that are approximately ½ inch (10 mm) in diameter.

2 Trace the design from the pattern section (page 162) and transfer it to a 13¾ x 17¾ inches (35 x 45 cm) piece of mountboard by re-drawing over the design.

3 Working one flower at a time, brush a thin coat of glue onto the board and fix the circles of rice paper in place so that they overlap the pencil lines of the design.

4 Create the four flowers shown in the picture above, working on one bloom at a time and referring to the guide on the page opposite for the placement of colors.

5 Tear the leaf shapes. Some have veins cut into them; make these by folding the leaf along its axis and cutting a thin slice from the folded edge with small scissors.

6 Glue each leaf to the mount board, smoothing the torn shapes into place. Glue the remaining flowers in position so that they slightly overlap the foliage.

TEARING THE PAPER

Hold the rice paper firmly between the thumb and forefinger of your left hand, pinch the paper with your right thumb and forefinger and tear from it a small circle.

WASHI CHIGIRI-E GLUING STAGES

*1. Brush glue over the section of
mount-board to be worked on
and apply the torn circles of
paper to form the flowers.*

*2. Continue to create the flowers
petal by petal, bloom by bloom.*

*3. Tear the leaf shapes and cut
the veins with scissors, then glue
them around the flowers.*

*4. Continue building up the
design, applying the petals so
they overlap the leaves.*

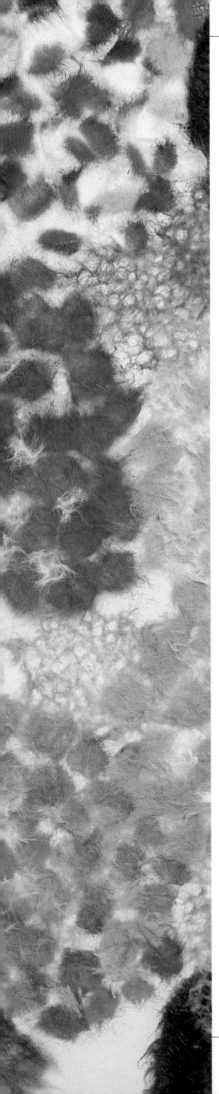

PAPIER-MÂCHÉ

THE TERM PAPIER-MÂCHÉ is French for 'chewed paper.' First used in the eighteenth century to describe the process that transformed waste paper into a hard-wearing material, the technique in fact predates its name by many centuries. Papier-mâché has long been used to make a variety of durable and often exquisitely decorated artifacts.

Papier-mâché tea caddy

A pulped paper substance was first used in the middle of the first millennium by the Chinese, who might be regarded as the first recyclers of paper. As the art of paper making spread via Asia to Europe, papier-mâché became an acceptable material out of which a wide variety of objects could be made. In India, beautifully painted and lacquered boxes, candlesticks, letter racks and other decorative items were produced.

During the eighteenth and nineteenth centuries, Europeans became fascinated by imported Chinese goods. An almost insatiable desire for *Chinoiserie* - a style of European art based on imitations of motifs in Chinese art - led to a demand in France and England for papier-mâché wares, especially objects decorated in the Oriental style. Factories were set up to cope with the demand, and the range of papier-mâché goods produced increased enormously.

The production of papier-mâché was revolutionized in 1773 by a process patented by Henry Clay. His method involved laminating long strips of paper together to make a cardboard-like material which could be stamped mechanically to produce items which were then painted and sealed. This laminated pasteboard was an effective replacement for wood, and the variety of items for which it was used included bookcases, screens, doors, chimney pieces and tables.

Persian barber's box

Papier-mâché is still used today for many purposes. Festivals frequently showcase masks and effigies made from the lightweight material. Its versatility, low cost and ease of use has made papier-mâché an indispensable material in many cultures, particularly Asian, Mexican and Southern European.

Papier-mâché is a popular material, suitable for items as large as tables or as small as boxes.

Painted and inlaid spirit case c. 1860

DESIGNS AND VARIATIONS

Papier-mâché is remarkable for its capacity to imitate other materials, such as clay, wood, stone and metal. Its paper-and-glue construction can be disguised by a simple coat of paint, or it can be emphasized by a roughness in the way the pulp or paper layers are built up. Whichever way it is used, the creative scope of papier-mâché is almost unlimited, and so is the scale. It is possible to create objects as large as a house, so long as a skeleton frame is provided, or to make items as small as buttons. The lightness and malleability of papier-mâché are two of its most remarkable qualities.

RAW MATERIALS

Recycle newspaper, tissue paper or any other paper that can be easily torn and molded.

MOLDS

A greased plaster mold like this fish-shaped one can be lined with newspaper strips and the shell removed when dry.

LAYERED POT

This pot is constructed with layers and rolls of paper and is painted to resemble earthenware.

JAPANESE FISH

A toy made with moveable fins demonstrates the playful side of papier-mâché.

COVERING CARDBOARD

Elaborate designs can be constructed from papier-mâché by covering cardboard shapes.

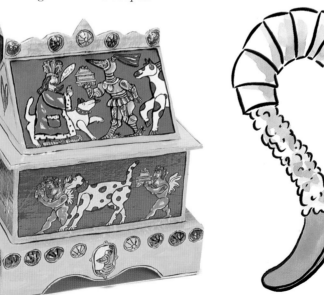

JUG HANDLE

Awkward shapes can be easily made with papier-mâché. To make this jug or mug handle, trace the shape onto cardboard, cut the shape out and cover with a thin layer of pulp. While still wet, wrap with strips of paper.

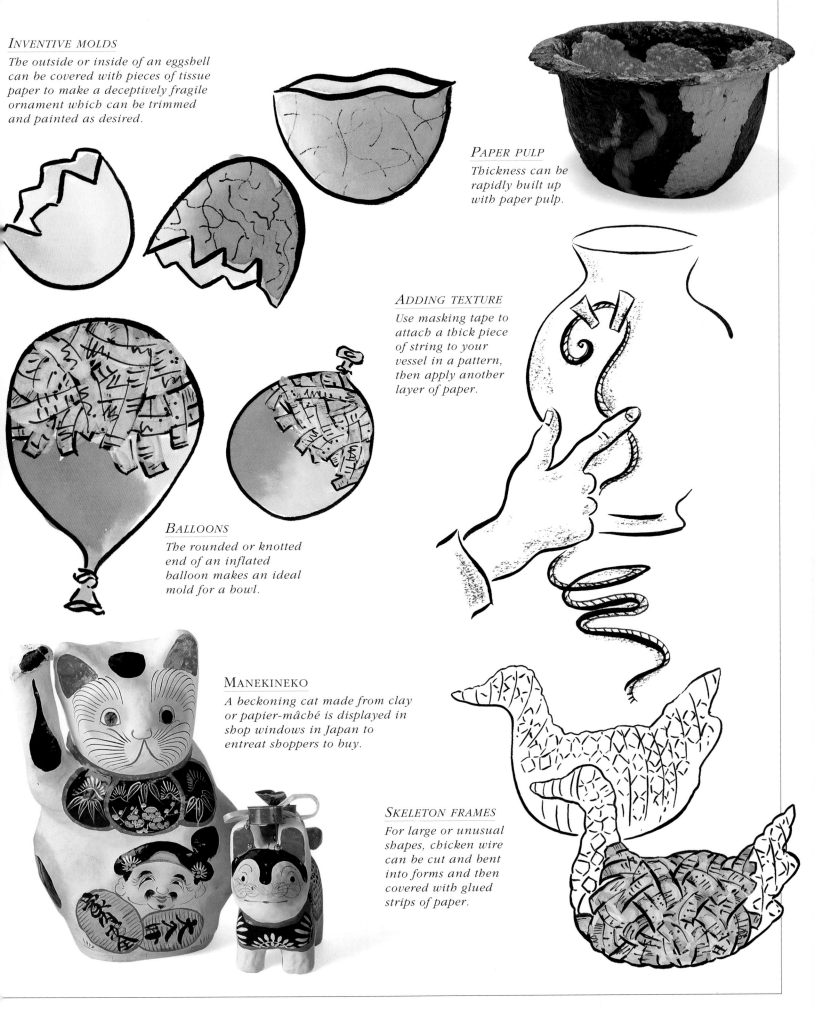

INVENTIVE MOLDS

The outside or inside of an eggshell can be covered with pieces of tissue paper to make a deceptively fragile ornament which can be trimmed and painted as desired.

PAPER PULP

Thickness can be rapidly built up with paper pulp.

ADDING TEXTURE

Use masking tape to attach a thick piece of string to your vessel in a pattern, then apply another layer of paper.

BALLOONS

The rounded or knotted end of an inflated balloon makes an ideal mold for a bowl.

MANEKINEKO

A beckoning cat made from clay or papier-mâché is displayed in shop windows in Japan to entreat shoppers to buy.

SKELETON FRAMES

For large or unusual shapes, chicken wire can be cut and bent into forms and then covered with glued strips of paper.

PROJECT: PAPIER-MÂCHÉ TRAY

Summer-bright colors and loose, confident brush strokes give a fresh finish to this papier-mâché tray. Made by gluing layers of paper strips into a mold and painting the dried shell, the finished object is a reminder that simple papercrafts can be as pleasing to the eye as more complicated ones.

Level of difficulty: Intermediate

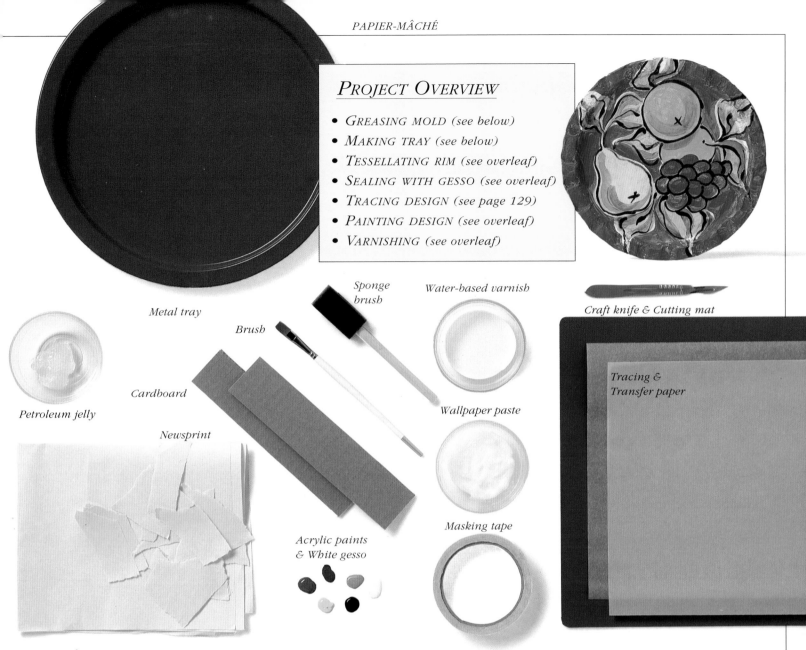

PROJECT OVERVIEW

- *GREASING MOLD (see below)*
- *MAKING TRAY (see below)*
- *TESSELLATING RIM (see overleaf)*
- *SEALING WITH GESSO (see overleaf)*
- *TRACING DESIGN (see page 129)*
- *PAINTING DESIGN (see overleaf)*
- *VARNISHING (see overleaf)*

Metal tray

Sponge brush

Water-based varnish

Craft knife & Cutting mat

Brush

Cardboard

Petroleum jelly

Newsprint

Wallpaper paste

Tracing & Transfer paper

Acrylic paints & White gesso

Masking tape

TRAY STEP-BY-STEP

1 Rub petroleum jelly over the upper surfaces of the metal tray, which forms your mold, in order to prevent the papier-mâché from adhering to the tray. Apply the jelly with your fingers.

2 Tear the paper into strips that are approximately 6 x 3 inches (15 x 8 cm) in size. Rub paste onto one side of the paper and line the mold with the strips. Apply 10 to 15 layers of paper.

3 Allow the papier-mâché to dry for a day then gently pry off the greased mold. Turn the papier-mâché piece upside-down onto a cutting mat and trim off the excess paper around the rim with a knife.

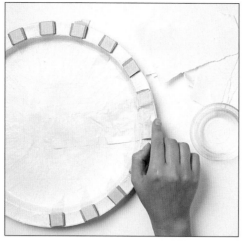

4 Cut small squares of cardboard of a size to fit comfortably around the rim of the tray. Space them at regular intervals and fix in place with masking tape.

5 Glue several more layers of paper to the tray, applying them first around the rim so that they fold over the edge, then to the center of the tray.

6 Allow the papier-mâché tray to dry for two or three days. Paint two coats of white gesso over all surfaces of the tray to create an even surface on which to paint.

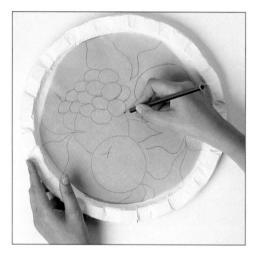

7 Trace the design (pattern page 163) and transfer onto the tray using carbon paper. The design will extend onto the rim of the tray; draw these lines in by freehand.

8 Paint the design, starting with the fruit and leaves then adding highlights in green. Paint the background and the back of the tray blue and add highlights to the grapes. Finish with black outlines.

9 Allow the paints to dry, then sponge an even coat of varnish over the surface of the tray, applying it first to the front and then to the back, allowing time to dry. Apply a second coat to both sides.

DETAILED VIEW

A minimum of 20 layers of paper is required to give the tray strength. The tessellated rim is made by gluing squares of cardboard onto the tray after the first 10 to 15 layers of paper have been applied, then covering them with more paper.

PAINTING THE DESIGN

Confident brushstrokes are the key to successful application of this design. Use a flat brush and paint each solid area with no more than a few strokes. Never apply the paint too thickly and leave some of the white gesso showing through, in order to bring out the fresh, translucent look of the colors.

1. Using the flat brush, paint the solid yellow, orange and purple colors of the fruit. Paint the leaves in light olive.

3. Paint the blue background around the fruit and leaves, applying the paint also to the back of the tray. Complete the design by outlining the shapes in black, using the flat brush.

2. Add green highlights to the leaves, oranges and pear using the flat brush. Give definition to the grapes with cobalt blue.

PROJECT: PAPIER-MÂCHÉ TREASURE BOX

Papier-mâché is often linked to memories of childhood, and this
treasure box, brightly painted with seaside motifs, captures the naive
charm of holidays remembered. The cardboard and papier-mâché
construction is simple and the design is easily rendered.

Level of difficulty: Intermediate

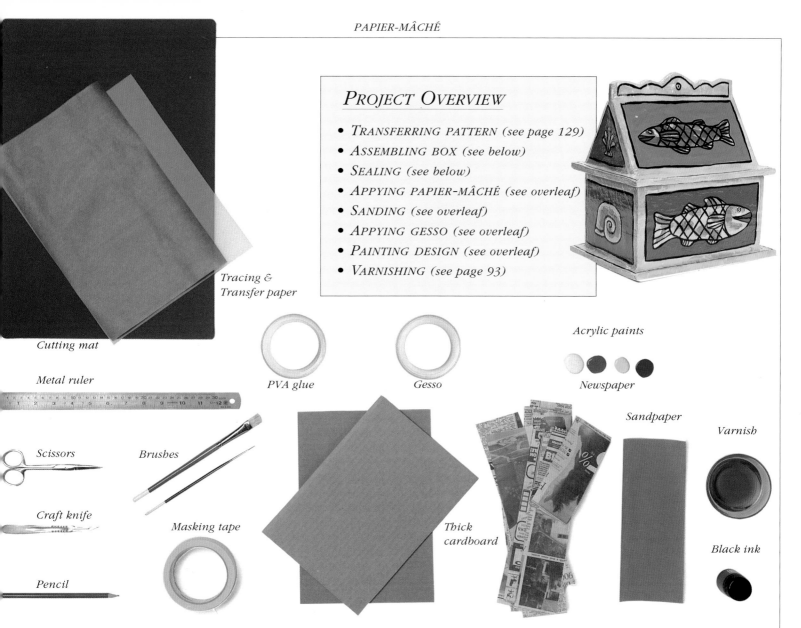

Tracing &
Transfer paper

PROJECT OVERVIEW

- TRANSFERRING PATTERN (see page 129)
- ASSEMBLING BOX (see below)
- SEALING (see below)
- APPYING PAPIER-MÂCHÉ (see overleaf)
- SANDING (see overleaf)
- APPYING GESSO (see overleaf)
- PAINTING DESIGN (see overleaf)
- VARNISHING (see page 93)

Cutting mat

Metal ruler

PVA glue

Gesso

Acrylic paints

Newspaper

Scissors

Brushes

Craft knife

Masking tape

Thick
cardboard

Sandpaper

Varnish

Black ink

Pencil

TREASURE BOX STEP-BY-STEP

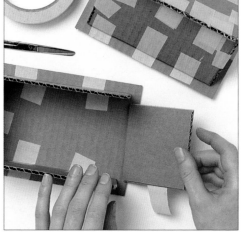

1 Trace the pieces for the lid and base (pattern page 165) and transfer them onto the cardboard. Using a craft knife, cut the pieces out against a cutting mat. Label the pieces so that they can be indentified.

2 Assemble the lid and base, using the photograph to the left as a guide to construction. Use PVA glue to join the pieces where they meet, then secure all the joints with pieces of masking tape.

3 Seal the lid and base, both inside and out, with PVA glue which has been diluted 50:50 with water. This will prevent the cardboard from warping when the papier-mâché is applied. Allow time to dry.

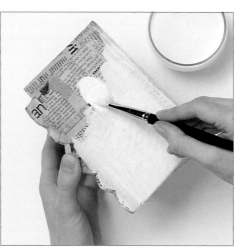

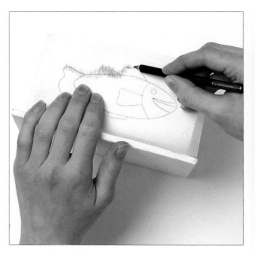

4 Cover the lid and box with strips of newspaper (see below). Leave to dry overnight in a warm place, but not too close to direct heat, then lightly abrade all surfaces with sandpaper.

5 Paint two coats of white gesso onto the lid and base, allowing time to dry between coats. The gesso primes the papier-mâché, providing a smooth surface on which to paint the design.

6 Trace the fish and shell designs (pattern page 164) and transfer them onto the outside surfaces of the box and lid, centering the designs so that their borders lie evenly within each plane.

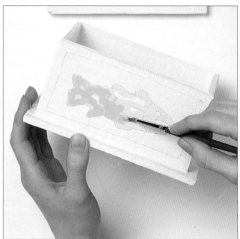

7 Dilute pale yellow paint with water to make a wash. Using a large round brush apply it to each of the motifs, leaving some areas of white showing.

8 Build up the design with darker tones of paint, applying the colors freely for a naive effect. Paint in the background colors last. Apply yellow paint around the edges as well as inside the box and lid.

APPLYING PAPIER-MÂCHÉ

Tear the newspaper into strips approximately 1¼ inches (3 cm) wide. Coat each strip with diluted PVA glue and apply to the lid and base, overlapping the strips slightly. Use smaller pieces to cover the curved gabling on the lid. Apply four layers of newspaper and allow the whole piece to dry thoroughly.

9 Allow the paints to dry, then add definition to the design by applying thin lines of black waterproof ink with a liner brush. Also paint border lines and emphasise the line of the gabling on the lid.

10 Apply two coats of gloss varnish to the inside and outside of the lid and the base, allowing the first coat to dry thoroughly before applying the second. To finish, fit the lid onto the box.

PAINTING THE DESIGN

The illustrations below indicate the painting stages for the yellow fish, but the same steps apply to the painting of the green fish and the sea shells. Always begin with pale colors and build up the intensity by applying stronger colors.

1. Paint a wash of yellow inside the outline of the fish, then apply a stronger mix of yellow, using free brush strokes.

2. Apply strokes of orange-yellow to the body of the fish. Paint the mouth and the background in red.

3. Highlight the fish by painting black lines around the main features. Use waterproof ink and a liner brush, and apply the ink in a fluid motion.

PAPER CUTTING

FOR AS LONG AS PAPER has been available it has been folded, cut and painted in countries as diverse as China, Mexico, North America, Poland and Germany. From crisp silhouettes and gaily colored doilies to lacy love vignettes and sacred pictures, papercuts have described the daily and seasonal activities of their makers, proving the craft to be one of everyday people.

Chinese paper cut

The Chinese not only invented paper, they were the first to incise it. In the production of embroidery patterns, window decorations and funerary gifts, papers were finely cut with knives and then painted using colorful inks. Itinerant craftsmen sold their work to a populace desirous of the good fortune and prosperity papercuts were believed to bring.

The European tradition of paper cutting is the younger relative of the Asian art, but its folklore is no less firmly established. German paper cutting, called *scherenschnitte*, was developed from the medieval monastic practice of cutting prayer pictures. At the peak of its popularity the finely slashed and stippled white paper sheets could be found decorating almost everything, from love letters to baptismal certificates. Many of the motifs found in *scherenschnitte* are now closely associated with the North American tradition, with such images as the tulip, eagle, heart and unicorn being popular.

Papercuts have long been used in decoration.

The images of *wycinanki*, the Polish form of paper cutting, were originally made using sheep shears. Brightly colored and stylized, these papers were pasted to ceilings and walls at Easter in celebration of the spring. The designs were cut from single squares of paper which, when opened out, had the look of fine lace doilies.

A style of paper cutting belonging to no fixed tradition is the silhouette. Alternatively known as shadow portraiture, this style of paper cutting has been practiced at least since Etruscan times, and its stark forms represent paper cutting at its boldest and most naturalistic.

Although removed in time, geography and cultural achievement, the many paper cutting traditions share a single heritage. Reflecting universal themes, papercuts are a poignant record of the lives of their makers.

An American silhouette from the 1930s

DESIGNS AND VARIATIONS

To the Chinese heritage of *huang-hua*, the Japanese tradition of *mon-kiri*, the German *scherenschnitte*, Polish *wycinanki* and the cross-cultural tradition of the silhouette, can be added papercut contributions from many other nations. The *papel picado* hangings and *amate* paper figures of the Mexicans and the naive papercuts of the American settlers confirm the universality of the paper cutting tradition.

POPULAR THEMES
The rooster appears in papercuts from China to Poland.

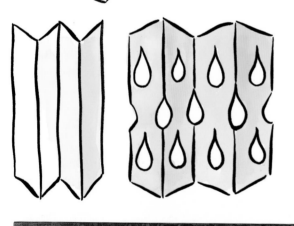

TOKENS
In North America, papercuts were given as love missives.

REPEAT PATTERNS
Using a pin to pierce a stack of papers will eliminate the need for multiple tracings.

FOLDING AND CUTTING
Folding before cutting saves time and produces symmetrical designs. The three folds shown are a concertina fold (left), a simple square fold (above) and a circle fold (below).

NAIVE ART
Stylization takes priority over realism in most papercut pictures.

CUTTING TECHNIQUES

Whether using scissors or a knife to cut a design, it is important to start by cutting the main shapes first and finish with the finer details.

SYMBOLIC CUTS

The glove, a symbol of faith and valiance, is cut with a heart design.

RELIGIOUS CUTS

Made from soft tissue paper and embellished with metal studs, papercut images like this were once cut with punches and given to young nuns to mark the end of their novitiate.

ASSEMBLAGE

Layering one or more papercuts on top of another to produce a collage is a Polish speciality.

CHINESE PAPERCUT

Originally used as stencils, Chinese papercuts became end products in themselves, like this old, hand-cut card.

THEMES FROM NATURE

A Swiss flower design chronicles a common preference for plant and animal motifs amongst paper cutters.

PROJECT: SCHERENSCHNITTE

Cut from a single sheet of white paper and intricately hand-painted, this papercut abounds with the stylized flower, foliage and animal motifs typical of the *scherenschnitte* tradition. The project is not difficult, requiring only time and a little patience.

Level of difficulty: Intermediate

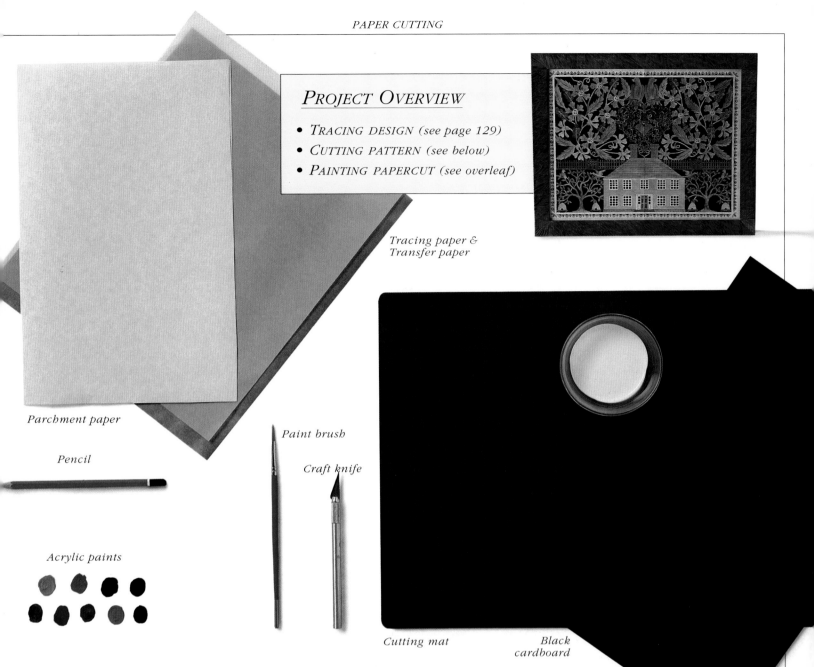

PROJECT OVERVIEW

- *TRACING DESIGN (see page 129)*
- *CUTTING PATTERN (see below)*
- *PAINTING PAPERCUT (see overleaf)*

*Tracing paper &
Transfer paper*

Parchment paper

Pencil

Paint brush

Craft knife

Acrylic paints

Cutting mat

*Black
cardboard*

SCHERENSCHNITTE *STEP-BY-STEP*

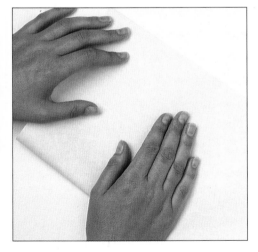

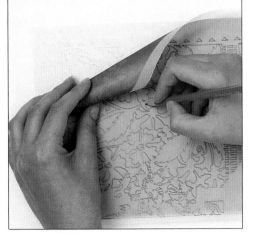

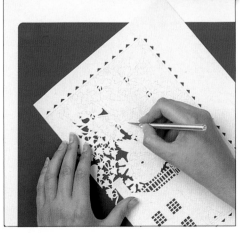

1 Fold a 15¾ x 11¾ inch (40 x 30 cm) piece of parchment paper in half so that the short sides meet. This halves your cutting time, since the design is symmetrical.

2 Trace the design (pattern page 166) onto tracing paper. Place a piece of transfer paper onto the parchment, then transfer the design from the tracing paper.

3 Place the parchment on a cutting mat and begin cutting from the center of the design, pulling the knife towards you and turning the paper as you work.

4 Continue cutting the design, working outwards from the center to the edges. A very sharp knife is important; replace the blade if the paper starts tearing.

5 Unfold the paper once the cutting is completed and begin painting, adding water to the paint to dilute it. Paint all areas of the same shade at once.

6 Add details in undiluted paint. When dry, glue the piece to black cardboard by applying tiny droplets of glue, section by section, and pressing down.

CUTTING SCHERENSCHNITTE

In order to prevent the paper from ripping, press a finger close to the point of the knife when cutting. Cut by turning the paper rather than the knife, while pulling the blade towards you. A sharp knife and a good light source are both important.

PAINTING STAGES

Nine acrylic paints make up the palette for this design, but do not be afraid to mix the colors; gradated shades bring greater subtlety to the finished design. Use a fine, round brush to apply the colors, diluting them to a wash for the larger areas and applying them in a more concentrated form when adding the details. To blend colors on the paper, apply the lighter shade first. While the paint is still wet, apply the darker color and use a wet brush to blend the paints where they meet.

Mix turquoise and apply to the body of the bird. While the color is still wet, paint the breast and wings in brown. Paint the ivy in diluted dark green and add opaque details in the same shade. Mix a red-brown for the hearts.

Apply mustard-yellow for the flower centers and purple for the berries. Mix a pale orange-brown for the flowers. Paint the leaves and stems green.

Paint solid blocks of mustard-yellow, tan and red-brown onto the house. Use a fine brush to add the details in brown paint.

Paint the trunk, branches and beehive stands in dark brown. Paint the hives mustard-yellow and the fence red-brown. Apply paint for the leaves and birds as before, keeping the paint watery.

PROJECT: SHELF LINER

This shelf liner uses a traditional pear tree motif which captures the naive charm of this most simple and appealing of papercrafts. By folding the paper prior to cutting, it is possible to create several images at once.

Level of difficulty: Beginner

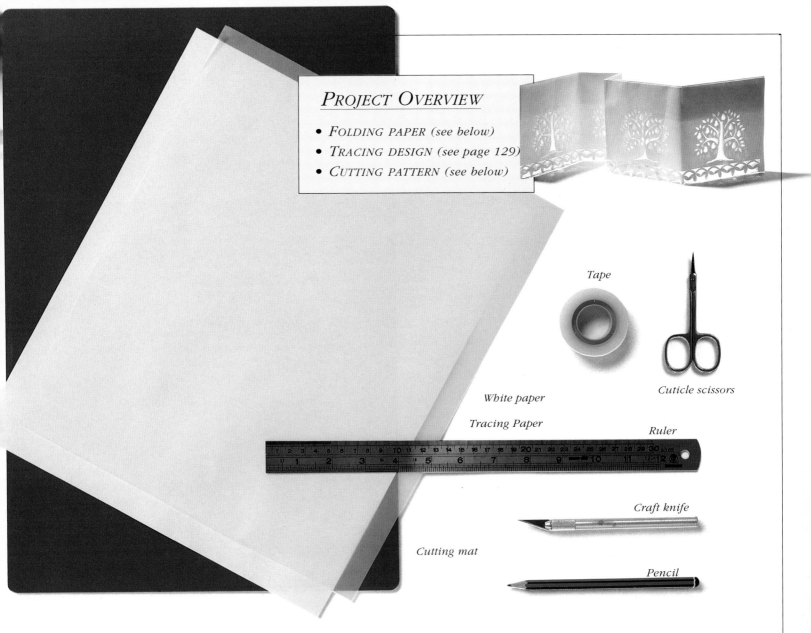

PROJECT OVERVIEW

- *FOLDING PAPER* (see below)
- *TRACING DESIGN* (see page 129)
- *CUTTING PATTERN* (see below)

Tape

Cuticle scissors

White paper

Tracing Paper

Ruler

Craft knife

Cutting mat

Pencil

SHELF LINER STEP-BY-STEP

1 Cut a 20 x 6 inches (48 x 15 cm) piece of white paper. Mark a line along the length of the sheet, 1½ inches (4 cm) in from one of the edges. Fold the paper in half lengthways so that the pencil line faces inwards, then fold in half again, aligning the edges perfectly.

2 Trace the design (pattern page 167) and insert the tracing behind the first leaf of the folded paper so that it shows through. Re-trace onto the shelf liner. Now cut the design with a craft knife; start with the tree trunk, then cut the foliage.

3 Cut the border design using small, sharp scissors to remove those parts which lie at the edge of the paper. Unfold the papercut and crease inwards along the line ruled in step 1. Cut as many papers as required to line a shelf, and tape in place.

103

PROJECT: SILHOUETTE

Silhouettes, otherwise known as shadow or profile portraits, are remarkable for their ability to capture a likeness in a few simple lines. Here, the late eighteenth century is vividly brought to life through the graceful lines and bold solids of silhouette portraiture.

Level of difficulty: Beginner

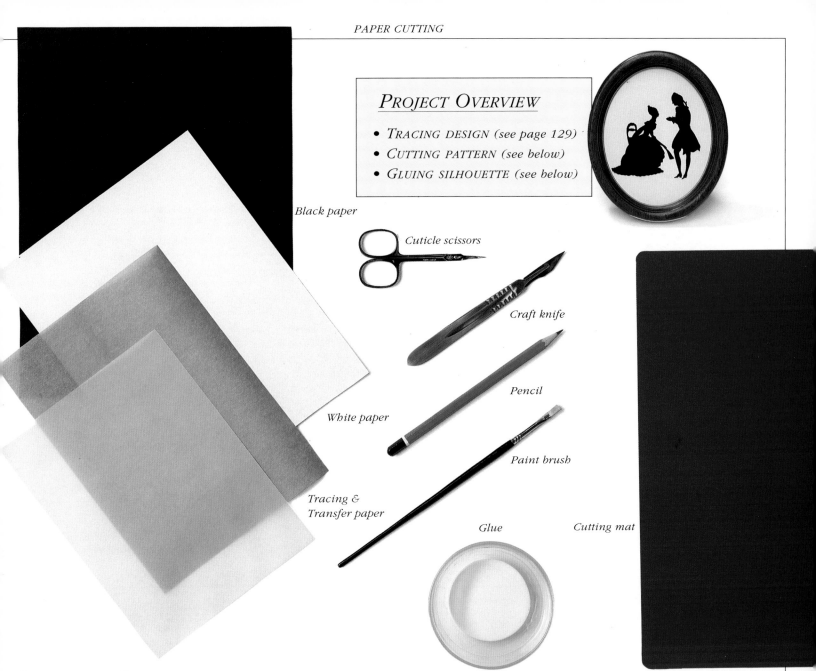

Black paper

PROJECT OVERVIEW
- TRACING DESIGN (see page 129)
- CUTTING PATTERN (see below)
- GLUING SILHOUETTE (see below)

Cuticle scissors

Craft knife

Pencil

White paper

Paint brush

Tracing &
Transfer paper

Glue

Cutting mat

SILHOUETTE STEP-BY-STEP

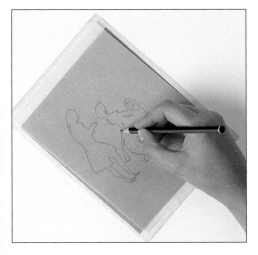

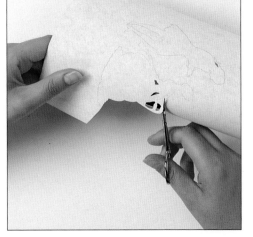

1 Trace the design (pattern page 168) and transfer onto the back of the black paper. Apply the pattern in reverse so that the image faces the right way when cut.

2 Use a craft knife first to cut the shapes inside the solid areas, then cut around the outlines of the figures using sharp scissors and making small, precise snips.

3 Mount the two silhouetted figures onto a piece of white paper, brushing a thin layer of glue onto the backs of the images and pressing them firmly in place.

QUILLING

FOLIAGE, FRUITS, GEOMETRIC PATTERNS, scroll work flowing and twisting its way through the design - all these have been formed with narrow strips of paper, rolled, shaped and placed on edge to form rich, intricate designs. At one time, the quills of birds or porcupines were used to create quilled work, hence the derivation of the craft's common name.

Quilled beads

The first evidence of the use of quilling comes from the churches and religious houses of the fifteenth century. Metal filigree work, which used gold and silver wire to decorate reliquaries, screens and panels, was common at this time, but paper rapidly proved itself to be a cheaper and more manageable substitute. Unskilled enthusiasts were able to create elaborate designs from paper strips which had been gilded or painted to resemble gold, ivory or other precious substances.

Nuns were responsible for creating nearly all the rolled paper work of the late medieval period. Narrow scraps of paper were obtained from the manuscripts illuminated by monks, and these trimmings were kept by the nuns for their art. In France, the Carmelite nuns were famous for their *paperoles* work, producing elaborate frames for holy pictures.

Quilling entered the secular domain during the Reformation, when it became a craft for genteel ladies. Workboxes, screens, furniture and even portraits were fashioned at this time. The strips of paper used were relatively wide, giving the designs a sculptural quality not found in later work.

A flowering of quilled work coincided with the Napoleonic Wars. In England it was deemed a suitable occupation for young girls, while in the jails, French prisoners of war made crude paper filigree boxes for entertainment. For the first time in its history, paper rolling expanded beyond the female domain and became a craft for both sexes.

Snowflake design

Quilling spread to North America with the settlers in the early nineteenth century, where the technique became more varied and the uses to which it was put diversified. Candle sconces were commonly decorated with colored papers which had been rolled, coated with wax and sprinkled with pieces of glass. From this time, the popularity of quilling rarely waned.

Special tools for winding paper strips have replaced the traditional quill, but the papers used today are the same as those of old.

Initialled box circa 1800

DESIGNS AND VARIATIONS

Quilling goes by many names - paper rolling, paper filigree, scroll work, mosaicon - and no less varied are the forms taken by the craft. Quilling can imitate gold and silver metal work, can be glued on edge on flat surfaces, arranged in free-form style or used to create three-dimensional objects. The scope is enormous.

RAISED QUILLING

The variety of quilling techniques includes three-dimensional work.

MINIATURE POTS

Rolled paper shapes on their own can be used to construct doll's house furniture and accessories.

STRUCTURAL WORK

The quilling technique can be applied with mediums other than paper, as shown by this basket, made from a whole tin can.

FRINGING & FEATHERING

Snip along the edge of a strip of paper before rolling it, or fringe around a pre-cut leaf shape for a feathery effect.

MINIATURE WORK

Strips of paper can be rolled and arranged on a small scale to make designs like this posy which is 1½ inches (4 cm) across.

WOVEN FILIGREE

Strips of colored paper can be woven to make baskets or other items.

QUILLING TOOL

The quilling technique used to make miniature pots and bluebells involves shaping the paper down the tool as it is wound to make a dimensional coil.

QUILLED BEADS

Paper strips cut from magazines take on the appearance of polished stones and shells when quilled.

FILIGREE FLOWERS

Quilled shapes lend themselves to floral designs like these.

DECORATIVE TOUCHES

An eighteenth century gilded frame, believed to commemorate a coronation, has red, white and blue silk pressed into some of its scrolls.

PROJECT: QUILLED BOX

In the past, delicate paper scroll work was coated with gold and
silver paint in imitation of metal filigree, but here it is exhibited in
all its subtle beauty. Pastel hues and intricate shapes reveal paper
in one of its finest forms through the elegant art of quilling.

Level of difficulty: Advanced

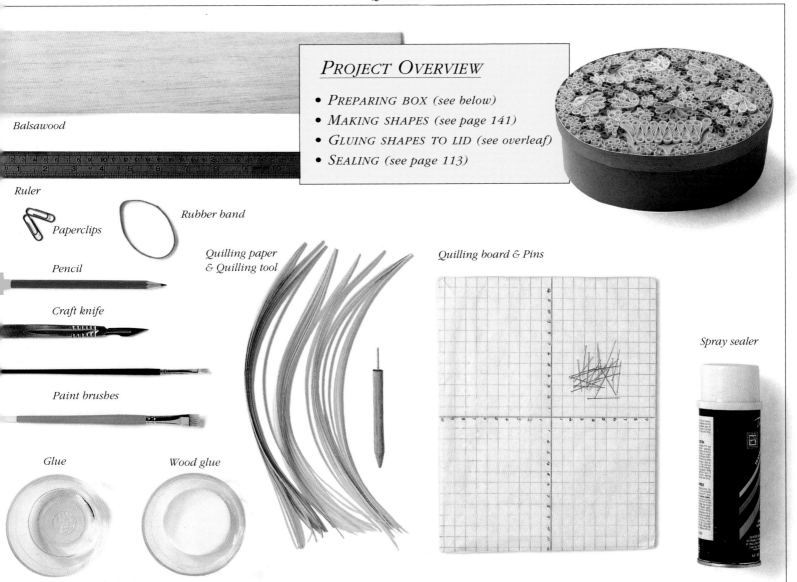

Balsawood

Ruler

Paperclips

Rubber band

Pencil

Craft knife

Paint brushes

Glue

Wood glue

Quilling paper & Quilling tool

Quilling board & Pins

Spray sealer

PROJECT OVERVIEW

- PREPARING BOX (*see below*)
- MAKING SHAPES (*see page 141*)
- GLUING SHAPES TO LID (*see overleaf*)
- SEALING (*see page 113*)

QUILLED BOX STEP-BY-STEP

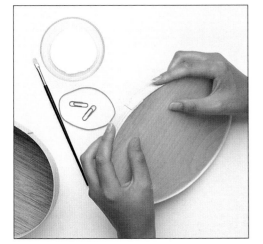

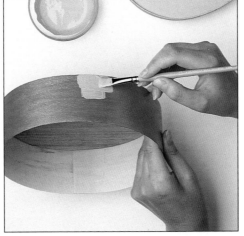

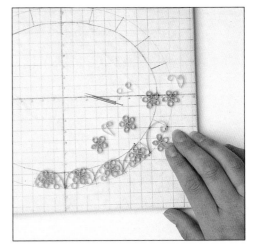

1 Make a ¼ inch (4 mm) lip on the lid of the box by cutting a piece of balsawood ¾ inch (2 cm) longer than the diameter and ¼ inch (4 mm) wider than the height of the lid. Glue into place, hold with paperclips and a rubber band until the adhesive is dry.

2 Paint two coats of pale green acrylic onto the lid and two coats of gold around its side. Paint the base of the box with gold, then brush on the crackle medium. Finish with another coat of pale green paint, which will crackle as it dries.

3 Prepare the quilled shapes (see page 141). Make a quilling board with a ½ inch (10 mm) grid (see page 145). Trace onto it the oval of the lid. Position the quilled border shapes onto the board, applying dots of glue and pinning to hold.

4 Complete the border. Allow the glue between the quilled shapes to dry, then brush a thin layer of glue onto the surface of the lid around the border area. Remove the pins and gently lift the border from the board. Place it onto the lid.

5 Join the remaining pieces for the center of the design, positioning them onto the quilling board and using pins to hold them in place while the glue dries. Refer to the design layout (page 169) for the placement of the various pieces.

6 Working piece by piece, apply glue to the back of each quilled shape and gently press onto the lid of the box. Start by gluing the larger floral pieces, then finish with the smaller filling shapes until the whole lid is covered.

DETAILED VIEW

The quilled shapes, once rolled, glued and joined together on the quilling board, are carefully removed, then attached to the lid of the box. Arrange the vase and floral pieces according to the photograph below. Place the filler shapes in the spaces to complete the design.

The border pieces are attached to the lid first, having already been glued together on the quilling board to make one large oval shape.

Glue the vase and flowers in place, applying glue to the back of the pieces and gently pressing in place.

Finish by inserting the filling shapes aound the main pieces, arranging them with an eye for color and spacing.

MAKING THE QUILLED PIECES

A gridded quilling board allows you to make uniform rolls to the correct size. Make the basic quilled shapes according to the instructions on page 141 using colored quilling papers of your own choosing, or refer to the detailed view of the lid on the opposite page.

7 When the glue has completely dried, apply spray sealer to the whole area of the lid. Spray the body of the box as well, inside and out. When the sealer has dried, place the lid on the box and tie a ribbon around the box for decoration.

Poppy: 5 teardrops & 1 crescent (make 5)

Border shapes: 5 small teardrops (make 20) & loose scrolls (as required)

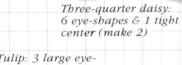

Three-quarter daisy: 6 eye-shapes & 1 tight center (make 2)

Vase piece: 15 small teardrops & 2 large petal shapes, placed inversely to each other (make 1)

Tulip: 3 large eye-shapes & 2 small diamonds (make 2)

Full daisy: 9 petal shapes & 1 tight roll center (make 1)

Filling shapes: 5 small teardrops, 3 eye-shapes & loose scrolls (as required)

CHINESE PAPERCRAFT

A VIGOROUS TRADITION of papercraft runs through China's history. Combining utility with beauty, paper has been crafted by ordinary people for domestic and public use for many centuries. Peasant farmers worked during the winter to produce intricate papercuts, bright lanterns and dramatic kites, drawing on a rich artistic heritage of symbols, motifs and legends for their designs.

Flat paper fan

Festivals marking the change of seasons have long been important to the Chinese, with many papercrafts being created especially for use during these celebrations. The Spring Festival provides the perfect opportunity for colorful pictures to be cut from thin sheets of paper. These papercut designs, called *huang-hua,* or 'window flowers', are pasted to walls and windows in celebration of the new season. Papercut patterns are handed down from one generation to the next and used as stencils for making porcelain, lacquer-ware and embroidery. Typical papercut designs include the peony, chrysanthemum, bat and butterfly. Colorful and bold, the images reflect aspects of the natural environment closely linked to the lives of their makers.

No celebration in China would be complete without paper lanterns. Originally designed to ward off bad spirits and bring prosperity, the brightly colored lanterns are still abundantly used for decoration today. A special Lantern Festival, held in the first month of the Chinese new year, used to be a showcase for lanterns of all descriptions. Usually made with waxed paper colored red, yellow or black, the more unusual lanterns took the shapes of plants, flowers and boats.

Kites have their origins in China. The Festival of Ascending on High fills the skies with kites of elaborate designs and vivid colors. Made from paper and silk, kites have been used in war and work, but today are built purely for pleasure.

Paper kite

The aesthetics of Chinese papercraft belong firmly to the folk art tradition. Far removed from the polished elegance of the palace crafts, Chinese paper creations are remarkable for their ebullience and simple beauty.

Paper lanterns sway in the breeze in a Chinese pergola.

A painted papercut, or huang-hua

DESIGNS AND VARIATIONS

The papercrafts of China are marked by a peasant flavor and a great vitality. Paper has traditionally been the material of the folk artist, whose love of the natural world manifests itself in a wealth of flower and animal designs. Heroes from Chinese history and theatrical figures from well-known stories also feature in paper designs, particularly in papercuts. Colors are bright, with an emphasis on the primaries. The Chinese outlook on life finds expression in the many beautiful paper designs that symbolize happiness, hope and peace.

PAPER LANTERNS
Elegant lanterns are cut and constructed from waxed paper.

PAINTED PAPERCUTS
Hand-cut with knives and then painted with brilliant inks, Chinese papercuts, featuring panda, lion and monkey designs, are often highly stylized.

CHINESE HERON
Papercuts are often displayed in windows and are called huang-hua, *or window flowers, even if they do not show floral motifs.*

116

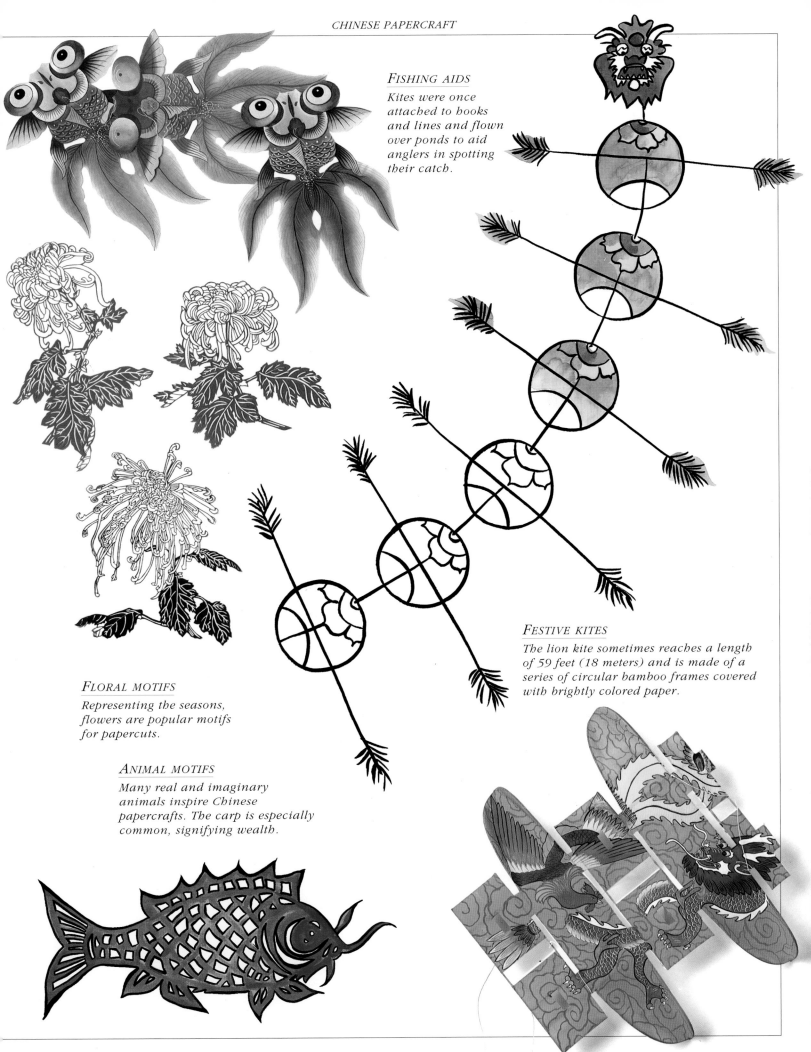

FISHING AIDS

Kites were once attached to hooks and lines and flown over ponds to aid anglers in spotting their catch.

FLORAL MOTIFS

Representing the seasons, flowers are popular motifs for papercuts.

ANIMAL MOTIFS

Many real and imaginary animals inspire Chinese papercrafts. The carp is especially common, signifying wealth.

FESTIVE KITES

The lion kite sometimes reaches a length of 59 feet (18 meters) and is made of a series of circular bamboo frames covered with brightly colored paper.

PROJECT: CHINESE KITE

The Chinese were flying elaborate, highly decorative paper kites as early
as the second century. This kite, with its long, dramatic tails and vivid
colors, is constructed on a traditional pattern. Called the Fertility Kite,
it makes spectacular viewing in flight or on land.

Level of difficulty: Advanced

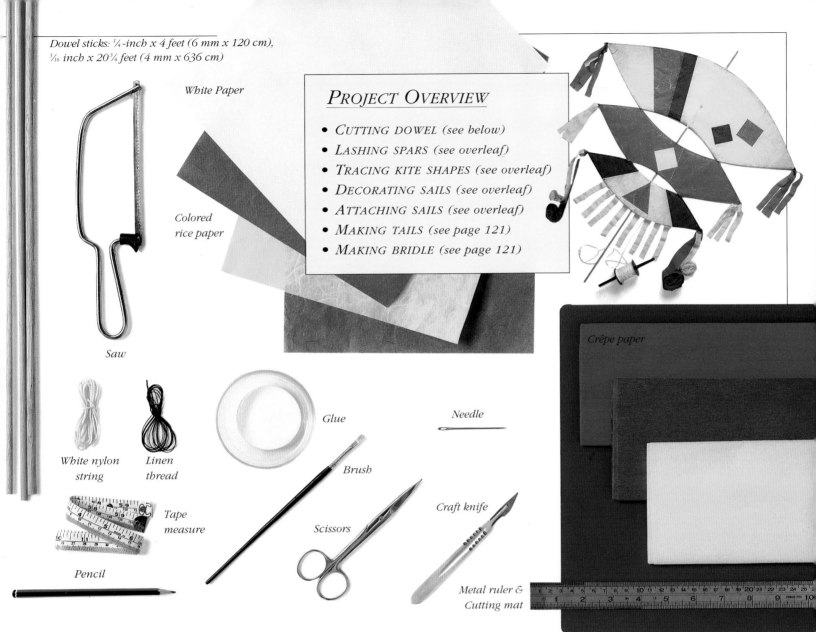

Dowel sticks: ¼-inch x 4 feet (6 mm x 120 cm), ³⁄₁₆ inch x 20¾ feet (4 mm x 636 cm)

White Paper

Colored rice paper

PROJECT OVERVIEW

- CUTTING DOWEL (see below)
- LASHING SPARS (see overleaf)
- TRACING KITE SHAPES (see overleaf)
- DECORATING SAILS (see overleaf)
- ATTACHING SAILS (see overleaf)
- MAKING TAILS (see page 121)
- MAKING BRIDLE (see page 121)

Saw

Crêpe paper

White nylon string   Linen thread

Glue

Needle

Brush

Tape measure

Scissors

Craft knife

Pencil

Metal ruler & Cutting mat

KITE STEP-BY-STEP

1 Refering to the measurements diagram on page 121, cut the spine and spars from lengths of dowel. Mark points A to G on the spine. Checking that the spars are centered, lash the two 4 feet (120 cm) lengths to the spine, at points A and D, with linen thread.

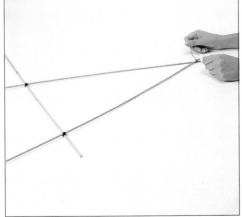

2 Pull the ends of the two spars together and lash with a length of thread (see overleaf for instuctions on how to lash). Lash the other ends of the cross-spars together in the same manner to make the first eye-shaped frame of the kite.

3 Turn the kite over and lash the two 3¾ feet (112 cm) spars to the spine at C and F. Turn the kite back over and lash the 2¾ feet (86 cm) spars at E and G. Lash the ends and the joints where each eye-shape meets the next. Brush glue over all the joints to secure.

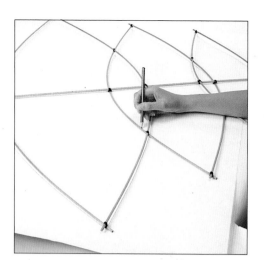

4 Lay the completed frame onto a large sheet of white paper and trace around the inside of each of the three large eye-shapes. Cut out, leaving a ½ inch (10 mm) allowance around each sail piece.

5 Lay the patterns on the colored rice paper and cut out. Cut decorative shapes of your choosing, then cut windows from the kite pieces, making them slightly smaller than the shapes. Glue in place.

6 Position the frame over the center piece of rice paper. Snip into the allowance at regular intervals, apply glue a little at a time, and roll the paper around the spars. Complete the remaining frames.

7 Cut kite tails from rolled crêpe paper: four 1½ foot (50 cm) lengths each of 1 inch (25 mm) wide green and yellow; two 8¼ foot (250 cm) lengths of 2 inch (50 mm) wide green; two 16½ foot (500 cm) lengths of 2 inch (50 mm) wide red; two 8½ foot (260 cm) lengths and eight 8 inch (20 cm) lengths of 1 inch (25 mm) wide yellow.

8 Use the 1½ foot (50 cm) lengths of 1 inch (25 mm) wide green and yellow to create the short, tufted tails. Lay two strips of the same color on top of one another and tie them together at their centers with linen thread. Tie to the tips of the two upper wings.

9 Join each of the red strips to the green to make two long tails. Lay the 8½ foot (260 cm) lengths of 1 inch (25 mm) wide yellow over the ends of the green and tie to the tips of the two lower wings. Glue the eight 8 inch (20 cm) yellow strips to the trailing edge of the kite.

LASHING

For lashing dowels, use thick linen thread and wet it before tying. As it dries, the thread will shrink to make a firm knot. Bind the thread in the form of a cross around the two dowels, then wrap the linen around each side of the dowel which lies underneath. Tie the ends of the thread in a square knot. As a final measure, coat all of the tied points on the completed frame with glue to ensure that the knots stay secure.

MAKING THE BRIDLE

Cut a 12 foot (360 cm) length of white nylon string. Attach it to point B on the spine by inserting a needle threaded with nylon string into the paper and lashing the string around the spine. Glue to hold. Attach the other end of the string to the spine at point G. To find the point at which to attach the flying line, lay the kite on the ground and pull the bridle upwards so that the string attached at point B forms a 90° angle to the kite. Tie the length of nylon cord for flying the kite at this point.

The spine is the main spar running from the top to the bottom of the kite. Cut a 4 foot (120 cm) length of ¼ inch (6 mm) dowel for this kite.

A. 4 inches (10 cm)

Spars are cut to create the framework. For the upper spars cut two 4 foot (120 cm) lengths of ⅙ inch (4 mm) dowel.

Decorative paper shapes enhance the beauty of the kite.

B. 11¾ inches (30 cm)

C. 15¼ inches (40 cm)

D. 1½ feet (50 cm)

A cylindrical spool allows you to unwind and wind the strong nylon line with ease and speed.

Middle spars: cut two 3¾ foot (112 cm) lengths of ⅙ inch (4 mm) dowel.

Bottom spars: cut two 34 inch (86 cm) lengths of ⅙ inch (4 mm) dowel.

E. 25½ inches (65 cm)

F. 27½ inches (70 cm)

From 2 inch (5 cm) wide crêpe paper cut two 33 foot (10 meter) lengths of green, two 16½ foot (5 meter) lengths of red and two 10 foot (3 meter) lengths of yellow. Glue one of each of the green, red and yellow lengths to each other to create two 59 foot (18 meter) tails. Attach them at point G.

G. 33½ inches (85 cm)

PROJECT: CHINESE LANTERN

Red is the color of joy and celebration in China, while lanterns
traditionally symbolize light and warmth. With such a happy union of
color and form, this colored paper lantern makes a delightful
decoration, perfect for creating a festive ambiance.

Level of difficulty: Intermediate

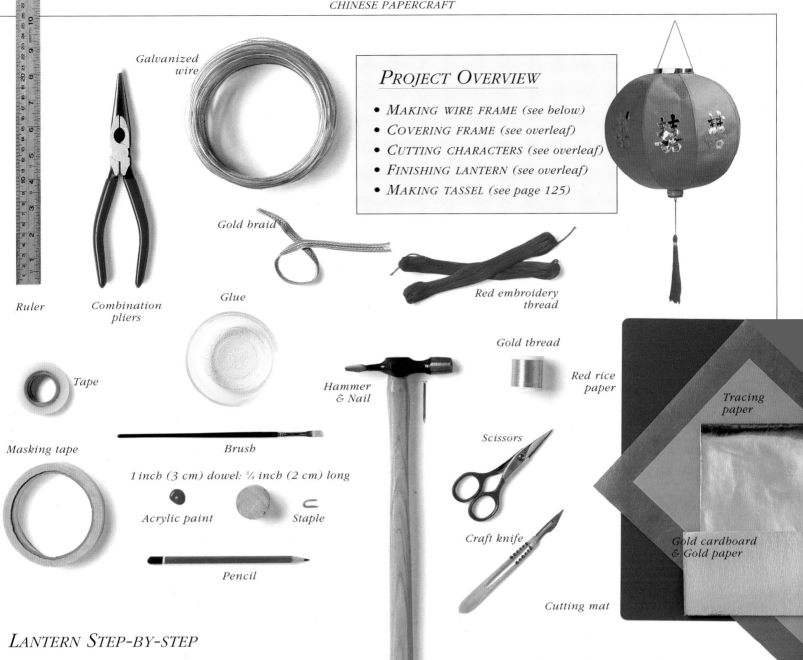

Galvanized wire

Ruler

Combination pliers

Gold braid

Glue

Red embroidery thread

Tape

Masking tape

Brush

1 inch (3 cm) dowel: ¾ inch (2 cm) long

Acrylic paint

Pencil

Staple

Hammer & Nail

Gold thread

Scissors

Craft knife

Cutting mat

Red rice paper

Tracing paper

Gold cardboard & Gold paper

PROJECT OVERVIEW

- *MAKING WIRE FRAME (see below)*
- *COVERING FRAME (see overleaf)*
- *CUTTING CHARACTERS (see overleaf)*
- *FINISHING LANTERN (see overleaf)*
- *MAKING TASSEL (see page 125)*

LANTERN STEP-BY-STEP

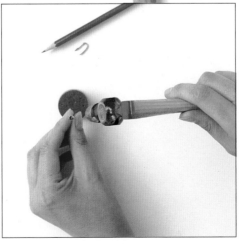

1 Cut a 27½ inch (70 cm) length of wire. Wrap it into a 3½ inch (9 cm) diameter circle and twist the ends. Wrap the frame with masking tape and mark eight evenly spaced points around the circumference.

2 Paint the dowel with two coats of red paint. On one side of the dowel make eight evenly spaced holes, about ⅛ inch (3 mm) deep, with a nail. Hammer the staple into the center of the other side.

3 Cut eight 15¾ inch (40 cm) lengths of wire. Shape the wire lengths into arcs by wrapping them around a large saucepan. Using pliers, bend ½ inch (10 mm) in from one end of each length to make a 90° angle.

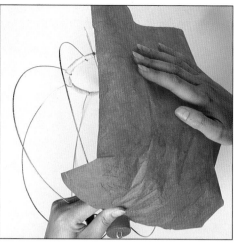

4 Insert the bent end of each length of wire into the holes. Lightly hammer to hold in place. Using pliers, bend the other end of each of the eight wires around the wire circle, attaching at the marked points.

5 From the red rice paper cut eight 15¾ x 5¼ inch (40 x 13 cm) rectangles. Using a brush, apply a coat of glue over two adjacent spines. Press one of the papers onto the spines, smoothing any wrinkles.

6 Cut the paper back to the spine but leave ½ inch (10 mm) at the top; apply glue and press it around the tape-covered circle. Cover every alternate segment and then the remaining segments in the same manner.

7 Cut eight 4¾ x 4 inch (12 x 10 cm) rectangles of gold paper. Trace the characters (pattern page 170) onto tracing paper and tape over the stack of gold paper. Cut with a craft knife.

8 Fix the Chinese characters to the lantern using only a little glue. Cut a 4¾ inch (12 cm) strip of gold braid and glue it around the dowel. Make the tassel (see opposite) and tie it to the staple.

FINISHING THE LANTERN

Tidy the edges where the paper segments meet by cutting ¹⁄₁₆ inch (2 mm) wide strips of rice paper and gluing them along each of the spines. For the hanging loop make a 11¾ inch (30 cm) length of braid from the embroidery thread. Glue the ends to the inside opening, at opposite sides. Cut a ¾ inch (2 cm) wide strip of gold cardboard that is 11¾ inches (30 cm) long. Tape it to fit the inside circumference of the top opening. Paint glue around the opening and insert the gold cylinder. Glue a second length of 11¾ inch (30 cm) braid around the top of the lantern where the frame meets the cylinder.

MAKING THE TASSEL

A tassel is easily made from a new, uncut skein of embroidery thread. Another 8 inch (20 cm) length is cut from the second skein for tying the tassel which, once completed, is attached to the staple in the dowel.

LOOPING THE THREAD

Separate the strands of the new skein to form a loop. Tie an 8 inch (20 cm) length of thread around the loop in a knot. Cut the loop with scissors at the opposite point to where it is tied.

TYING THE LOOP

At a point ¾ inch (2 cm) below the knot, tie a strand of gold thread around the tassel. Knot securely.

DECORATING

Tightly wrap a 10 inch (25 cm) length of gold thread around the top of the tassel to form a ¼ inch (6mm) wide gold band.

PROJECT: CHINESE PAPERCUT

Papercuts are used in China as decorations for lanterns and fans, as patterns for embroidery, and as colorful window displays. Here, a traditional design is cut and glued to cardboard to make a card. Several sheets can be cut at once with this simple technique.

Level of difficulty: Intermediate

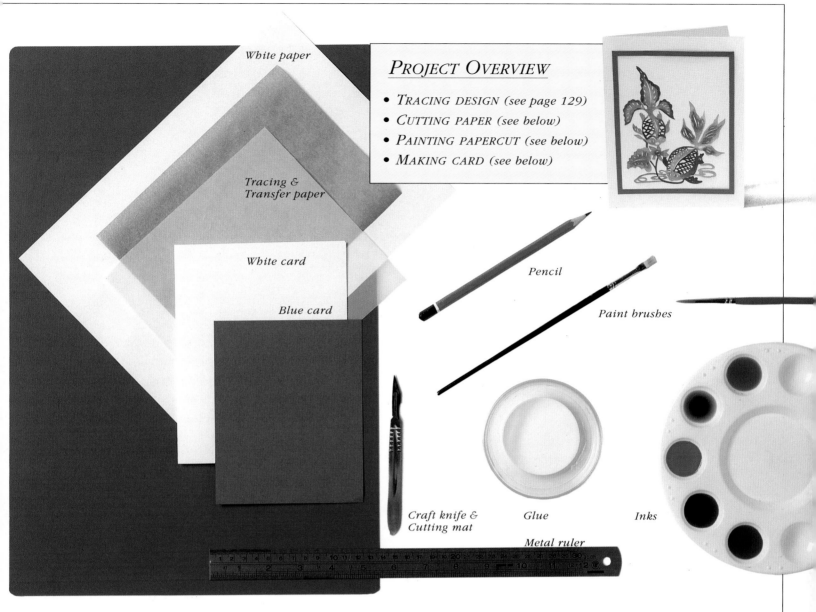

White paper

Tracing &
Transfer paper

White card

Blue card

PROJECT OVERVIEW

- *TRACING DESIGN* (see page 129)
- *CUTTING PAPER* (see below)
- *PAINTING PAPERCUT* (see below)
- *MAKING CARD* (see below)

Pencil

Paint brushes

Craft knife &
Cutting mat

Glue

Inks

Metal ruler

PAPERCUT STEP-BY-STEP

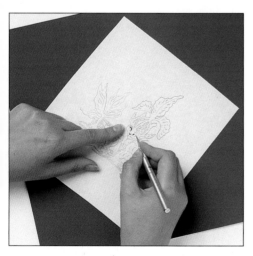

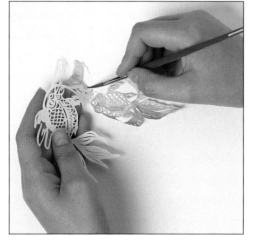

1 Trace the design (pattern page 170) and transfer onto white paper. Working on a cutting mat, cut out the design with a craft knife. Remove the inside shapes first, then cut around the outline.

2 Work carefully, turning the paper rather than the blade. When finished, paint with inks. Use a soft brush and apply the colors undiluted. Refer to the page opposite for the placement of colors.

3 Cut a 11 x 7 inch (28 x 18 cm) piece of white cardboard. Cut a ½ inch (10 mm) frame from blue card, the opening of which is 5½ x 4⅓ inches (14 x 11 cm). Glue to the card, then attach the papercut.

GENERAL INFORMATION

THE IMMENSE VARIETY OF PAPERCRAFTS is matched by an equally great range of papers. Deciding which paper to use for a particular craft project requires knowledge of your raw material. The textures and strengths of various papers lend themselves naturally to certain crafts, while others are less obviously appropriate, or suggest a number of uses. This chapter explains the qualities of paper and offers suggestions for ways of using and caring for it.

SUITABILITY OF PAPERS

Paper is a commonplace material, but its properties are often misunderstood. A knowledge of the way paper is constructed should lie behind any creative endeavor.

Paper consists of the interlaced fibers of plant material which has been shredded, broken down by boiling to release the cellulose in the fibers, then pulped and mixed with water. By draining this mixture through a sieve, a layer of fibrous material is collected. This, when dried, forms a sheet of paper.

When choosing papers, some factors to consider are the weight, strength, texture and color of the material. Aesthetics play only one part in the decision; whether paper meets the physical requirements of the intended project is of equal importance. Other variables, such as whether paper has been coated with size and what its pH is may have to be taken into account as well. Whole sheets that require wetting, such as in marbling, need to have a good wet strength. The two most important points to consider are the grain direction and the weight of the paper.

GRAIN

Handmade paper has randomly positioned fibers, unlike machine-made paper which has its fibers running in one direction. This difference affects the strength and flexibility of paper. The longer the fibers, the stronger will be the paper. Moreover, paper will fold and tear more easily along the grain and have a greater strength in the opposite direction. See page 140 for information on finding the grain.

Cutting and folding are the two most common techniques employed with paper.

Designs can be scaled up or down in size to suit the dimensions of a frame.

WEIGHT

Paper comes in a number of thicknesses, or weights. For projects that require strength from the papers they use you should choose heavier paper or cardboard. The skeleton structures of many projects are made from cardboard, for example the papier-mâché box and the stationery box. The heavier the paper, the less flexible it will be. It is important to weigh the relative merits of strength and flexibility when choosing papers for a particular project. Always use strong paper when mounting papercuts.

CUTTING

In many projects it is of great importance that design elements be measured and cut accurately. Even a small error can cause great frustration, or even the failure of your project. Projects such as the stationery box and kite require such precision at the initial stages. Always use a metal ruler when cutting straight lines. Place your paper on a cutting mat and hold the ruler along the line to be cut. Run the knife blade along the length of the ruler, close up against it. Ensure that your knife is sharp, and replace the blades when they become dull.

TRANSFERRING PATTERNS

Some of the designs contained within the pattern section will need to be enlarged. The easiest way to do this is to use a photocopying machine and enlarge by the required percentage. Alternatively, transfer the design onto tracing paper and draw a grid over it, numbering each square of the grid. Take another, larger piece of tracing paper and draw up a grid which is larger than the first by the percentage indicated. (If, for example, the pattern asks you to increase it by 130%, your second grid will be 1.3 times the size of the first.) Copy the details from the original tracing onto the enlarged grid, square by square. Tape the tracing in place where you require it, then insert a sheet of transfer paper between the tracing and the surface, with its coated side facing downwards. Retrace over the design with a stylus.

CARING FOR PAPER

Paper is a perishable material, but its life can be extended in a number of ways. Choosing good quality, acid-free paper is a first step. Most paper is made from wood pulp, which is naturally acidic. Left untreated, it deteriorates rapidly. Chemical treatment neutralizes the acidity, giving the paper improved strength and longevity. Papers with a high content of cotton or linen also have a longer life span and will not fade or yellow.

Once paper has been crafted, there are several steps which can be taken to prolong its life. Handmade papers can be coated with size to improve their strength and water-resistance, quilled designs can be sprayed with sealer for strength, papercuts can be mounted behind glass on acid-free board for protection. Other crafts, simply by their nature, preserve the papers from which they are made. Varnish ensures the preservation of découpage papers, for example, while the glue which binds papier-mâché together acts as a strengthening agent.

Other measures which prevent paper from perishing too rapidly include keeping it away from direct sunlight, spraying it with insecticide and avoiding handling the raw or finished paper product.

PAPER TYPES

A vast array of papers are on the market today, and though most of them are manufactured for the printing and packaging trades, there are a few basic types with which the paper artisan ought to be familiar.

CARDBOARD
A stiff-bodied material which is thicker than paper, usually made from rags or wood fiber. Cardboard is a versatile material, often used as a base for other crafts, such as box making.

COVER PAPER
A good quality paper, finely ridged on one side and available in a range of thicknesses and colors. Cover paper takes paint well and has a good wet strength.

NEWSPRINT
The unprinted material used for newspapers, it is inexpensive and excellent for papier-mâché. When macerated or layered and shaped into forms, it dries into a strong material.

CRÊPE PAPER
A tissue-like paper which is thin, crinkled and usually brightly colored. Crêpe paper has a distinct grain and texture and can be easily stretched and molded.

PARCHMENT PAPER
A paper resembling the authentic material made from the skin of goats. Parchment paper has a crisp texture and a heavy weight, making it suitable for cutting and painting.

JAPANESE PAPERS
The textures and colors vary enormously, with chiogami, razak *and* momijami *being among the more common papers. Made from bark fibers, they yield thin, strong papers.*

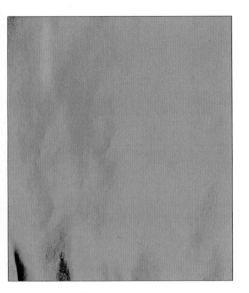

METALLIC PAPER
Papers and boards made with a metallic or plastic finish. Commonly available in gold and silver, these papers are usually cut up and used as trimmings on craft projects.

HANDMADE PAPER
Any paper which is made without the aid of machinery. Handmade paper bears the distinctive textures and structures of its raw materials and the mold on which it was formed.

TISSUE PAPER
A very thin, almost transparent paper, frequently used for wrapping delicate items. Its fragile, decorative qualities make it suitable for applications where it will not easily get damaged.

PRINTED PAPER
Paper which has had inked plates, blocks or type applied to it. The huge range of images available in books, magazines and other items provide a rich source for découpage.

MOUNTBOARD
A cardboard used in picture framing. Acid-free mountboard will not yellow or deteriorate quickly and has improved strength, making it ideal as a base pulp in paper making.

UNRYUSHI PAPER
A Japanese rice paper, known as ' dragon in the cloud.' Made with exceptionally long leaf and bark fibers, it is robust yet also pliant and translucent.

MATERIALS

QUILLING TOOL
Used to coil lengths of paper.

PIPETTE
Controlled quantities of a liquid can be added with a pipette.

PROBE
Used in Turkish marbling to drag paints into pictures.

CRAFT KNIFE
A craft knife with replaceable blades and a comfortable handle is suitable for cutting paper.

CUTTING MAT
Protects surfaces from cuts and lengthens the life of blades.

MIXING JARS
For mixing and storing paints and other liquids.

TRANSFER MATERIALS
Copy a pattern onto tracing paper and transfer with black carbon paper.

BONE FOLDER
When making a crease in paper, a bone folder can be used to create a sharp, clean edge.

MASKING TAPE
Used invisibly to hold components together in a reliable and flexible bond.

NEEDLE & THREADS
Good quality cotton and linen threads provide the strength required for papercraft projects.

PVA GLUE
A clear-drying glue, used where extra strength is required.

COMBINATION PLIERS
Wherever wire has to be cut or bent, use combination pliers.

METAL RULER
For measuring and cutting against, in preference to a plastic ruler which can be easily damaged by a blade.

PASTE
Suitable for joining pieces of paper together.

RIVETTER
For fastening eyelets to an object.

WHISK
A whisk is used for splattering paint evenly over the marbling size.

PENCIL
For marking measurements and patterns.

CRAFT GLUE
Used as a quick-drying adhesive.

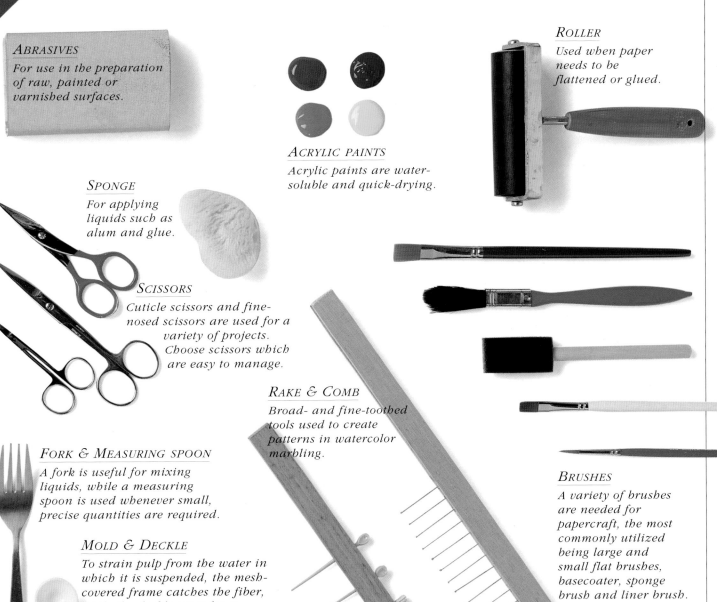

ABRASIVES
For use in the preparation of raw, painted or varnished surfaces.

ACRYLIC PAINTS
Acrylic paints are water-soluble and quick-drying.

ROLLER
Used when paper needs to be flattened or glued.

SPONGE
For applying liquids such as alum and glue.

SCISSORS
Cuticle scissors and fine-nosed scissors are used for a variety of projects. Choose scissors which are easy to manage.

RAKE & COMB
Broad- and fine-toothed tools used to create patterns in watercolor marbling.

FORK & MEASURING SPOON
A fork is useful for mixing liquids, while a measuring spoon is used whenever small, precise quantities are required.

MOLD & DECKLE
To strain pulp from the water in which it is suspended, the mesh-covered frame catches the fiber, while the deckle provides a frame for the fiber, giving a sheet of paper its shape.

BRUSHES
A variety of brushes are needed for papercraft, the most commonly utilized being large and small flat brushes, basecoater, sponge brush and liner brush.

PAPER MAKING

GENERAL INFORMATION

Most handmade paper is made either from plant fiber (which includes cotton and linen rags), recycled paper, or a combination of the two. Almost any plant which has strong cellulose fibers can be turned into paper through a process of shredding and softening.

The best quality recycled material to use in handmade paper is acid-free mountboard, obtainable from picture framing shops as scrap. Office or computer paper also makes good quality pulp, but avoid newspaper as it is acidic and has short fibers, resulting in a finished paper of poor quality.

Leftover pulp can be stored in sealed containers for up to two weeks, or in a freezer indefinitely. Drain excess water from the pulp before you store it in order to reduce its bulk.

PREPARING RECYCLED PAPER PULP

Tear up mountboard or other paper into small pieces and soak for at least 24 hours in a bucket of cold water. (Half a bucket of shredded mountboard will make approximately 30 standard sheets of paper.)

Paper is torn into pieces, soaked in water and then blended to a pulp prior to paper making.

Pour water into a blender until it is three-quarters full. Add a small handful of wet mountboard pieces and blend for a few minutes to a creamy pulp. To determine whether the pulp is beaten enough, fill a small glass jar with water, add a little pulp and stir well. If the suspended fibers are well dispersed with no lumps or pieces of paper visible, the pulp is ready. If not, blend until there are no lumps.

When all the pulp has been blended it is ready to use to form your handmade sheets of paper.

PREPARING PLANT FIBER

Collect about 7 oz (200 g) of plant fiber and cut into ¾ inch (2 cm) pieces using scissors or garden clippers. Soak in water for about 12 hours.

Fill a stainless steel pot with sufficient water to cover the plant fiber, but do not add the fiber yet. Heat the water, and just before it boils, prepare the caustic soda (also called lye). It is essential to wear rubber gloves and protective clothing at any time when handling caustic soda. Take care not to splash caustic on your skin; rinse immediately with cold water if an accident occurs. The quantity of caustic soda required is about 10% of the dry fiber weight, therefore for 7 oz (200 g) of fiber you will need ¾ oz (20 g) of caustic soda. Weigh the quantity of caustic and stir it into a small glass jar of cold water. Never add water to the caustic soda, as it will bubble and possibly splash.

Before the water comes to the boil, add the caustic solution and then the fiber. Simmer for three hours or longer, stirring every half hour. The fibers are ready if they come apart easily when pulled with a fork. Drain off the remaining caustic solution, diluting it with plenty of water or adding vinegar to neutralize it.

Place the fiber in a strainer and rinse it until the water becomes clear. Alternatively, let the fiber soak in a bucket of water and change the water every hour or so. When the fiber is completely clean, it can be beaten in a blender in the same way as recycled paper pulp.

To shorten the boiling and beating processes, it is possible to first partially break down fibers by allowing them to ferment for a few weeks. Place chopped plants into a bucket, cover them with water and seal. Leave the bucket in a warm place for as long as necessary for the plants to rot, then boil with caustic (preferably outside, as the decomposed fibers will smell) and beat to make a pulp.

SIZING

Inks and paints will not bleed or run if they are used on paper which has been sized. Size is a weak glue which can be applied to the surface of seasoned paper or added to the vat during paper making.

When using size in the vat, the pulp must not be too acidic or the paper will discolor and become brittle. A pH of 7 is considered neutral and can be measured with a pH indicator. After couching the paper, it is important to rinse the pieces of felt to prevent them from stiffening when they dry. Those sizes which can be applied directly to the surface of paper can be applied either with a spray bottle or with a soft paint brush. See page 15 for size recipes.

Plant fiber is cut into short lengths, boiled with caustic soda and strained with a sieve.

COUCHING

Once a sheet of paper has been formed on the mold, the deckle is lifted away and the sheet transferred onto a piece of fabric. It is then pressed between boards to drain away as much water as possible. Sophisticated paper making methods use a book press, but a perfectly satisfactory press can be made from boards held together with clamps. Lay down a board which is slightly larger than your sheet of paper. On top of the board lay a damp piece of thick felt or blanket, then a damp piece of cotton fabric. Roll the paper off the frame (see page 14) and

onto the fabric, then place another damp cloth on top. Continue forming sheets of paper and placing damp cloths on top of them until the pile contains between 20 and 30 sheets of paper. Finally, lay down another piece of felt or blanket and then another board. Apply clamps to the top and bottom boards, at either side, and tighten them. Turn the couching pad on its side to allow the water to drain away.

Sheets of cotton fabric and felt are held between boards with clamps to make the couching pad.

MARBLING

GENERAL INFORMATION

There is no single formula for mixing marbling colors. Water quality, surface tension, pigment opacity and a variety of other factors will determine the proportions of the ingredients to be mixed. The best way to proceed, therefore, is to add the ingredients little by little, testing the mix on the surface of the size.

The ideal watercolor marbling pigment is a water-based paint, ground specifically for marbling, but gouache and watercolor paints can also be used. Water used for diluting the paints should be soft, preferably distilled. An ingredient added to the paint is ox gall, a bile extracted from the gall bladder of cows. Ox gall is a surfactant, or surface-active substance, which causes the paint to float on the surface of the size. In addition, it gives the colors a fatty coating to prevent them from blending into one another. Marbling suppliers and some art shops stock ox gall.

Oil color marbling does not require such careful preparation as watercolor marbling. Although oil color marbling uses the same equipment as water-color marbling, it is not advisable to use the same tray and tools, as oils can contaminate the watercolor process, even if the tray has been well cleaned.

MIXING & TESTING WATERCOLORS

Before blending the ingredients, prepare a tray of size (not your marbling tray) on which to test the paints. A small baking pan is suitable for this purpose.

Mix the paints in jars, starting with one tablespoon of pigment and adding water until the paint is the consistency of milk. Add one drop of ox gall and mix thoroughly with a fork. Skim the pan with newspaper, then add a few drops of color. If the paint sinks, add another drop of ox gall, skim the surface and try again. The correct consistency has been achieved when the paint floats and spreads out into a circle about the size of an egg yolk. If the paint spreads too far, add some more paint and test again.

Repeat the mixing and testing process for each color intended for use, then test the colors together to check that they float and spread when they share the same surface. Each color laid will need more ox gall than the one previous to it if you want the paints to spread in equal amounts. The first color laid will be the most compressed and the last will be the most dominant. The order in which you test the colors now should be the same order in which they are dropped on to the tray prior to making a print.

Ox gall tends to dilute colors, making them paler, so you may wish to make colors stronger at the initial mixing stage.

Ox gall and water are mixed with watercolor paints, while oil colors require only mineral turpentine to dilute them.

Alum is mixed with hot water, allowed to cool to room temperature and applied to paper with a sponge.

MIXING & TESTING OIL COLORS

Artist's paste oils are suitable for oil color marbling. For metallic colors use enamel paints, which are available from hardware stores.

Into a glass or metal container place two tablespoons (50 g) of oil paste color. Stir in enough mineral turpentine to bring the mixture to a milky consistency.

Prepare a tray of size (see below) to test your colors on. Oil colors are not likely to sink in the way that watercolors are, but the way they disperse can be unpredictable. Apply drops of color to the size. If a color refuses to spread, forming tiny droplets instead, add more turpentine to the paint. Alternatively, try applying colors in a different sequence, as some are more compatible than others.

MAKING A MARBLING SIZE

In order for both watercolor and oil color paints to float, the liquid on which they are dropped must be thickened. This is called the size. The most effective sizing agent is a gum derived from carrageenan moss, a type of seaweed. Carrageenan is available in a powdered form from marbling suppliers.

To mix the size, use the proportions of one tablespoon of carrageenan to every 2 quarts (2 liters) of water. Fill a blender three-quarters full with tepid water, add half a tablespoon of carrageenan and blend thoroughly. Pour the size into a bucket and repeat the blending process for the rest of the carrageenan. Add enough water to the bucket to make up the required quantity, cover it and let it sit covered for a minimum of eight hours, or preferably overnight. (A standard tray holds 4½ gallons (20 liters), for which quantity you would use six to eight tablespoons of carrageenan.) Pour the size into the marbling tray before applying paints to the surface.

Once it has been mixed with water, carrageenan size will only keep for a number of days, so only make enough size for the project at hand. Washing soda can be used as a preservative. Dissolving one teaspoon into 4½ gallons (20 liters) of water will preserve the size for two weeks or longer.

MAKING AND APPLYING ALUM

To permanently fix marbling colors, a mordant is applied to the paper to be marbled. A mordant is a chemical that combines with a dye to form an insoluble compound. For marbling, use aluminum, or 'alum,' as it is known. Alum comes in three different crystalline salts: aluminum sulphate, potassum aluminum sulphate and ammonium aluminum sulphate. All are equally suitable mordants for paper marbling.

When mixing and applying alum, wear rubber gloves for protection. Make an alum solution by dissolving two tablespoons (50 grams) of the aluminum sulphate you have chosen into half a quart (1 liter) of hot water. Stir until dissolved and allow to cool to room temperature.

Lay a piece of paper onto a flat surface and mark the side which is to be coated with mordant. As the alum dries clear it is difficult to distinguish which side of the paper has been coated; the mark will indicate which side to marble. Dip a sponge into the alum solution, ring it out and spread the mordant evenly over the entire surface using vertical, overlapping strokes, then horizontal ones. The paper should be damp, not wet, and stacked six to eight sheets at a time on top of one another. These should be placed between heavy sheets of cardboard, larger than your paper size. Cover the stack of papers with a varnished board and place a heavy weight on top. The papers can be stored in this way, ready for several days' marbling.

DÉCOUPAGE

SEALING

Coating the cut paper images with sealer before gluing them down protects them from tearing and prevents the varnish from penetrating the paper and discoloring the prints. Sealer can also give body to thin papers and discourage them from curling at the edges once they have been cut out. However, do not seal papers which are to be adhered to curved surfaces, as the sealer can stiffen them too much, making them hard to bend. Applied to raw wood, sealer also provides a non-porous working surface. PVA glue is effective when used undiluted.

GLUING

Acrylic-based glues are generally the most suitable ones to use for découpage. PVA glue can be used undiluted for images that can be quickly applied, or diluted with paste for more complex areas to slow the drying time.

Apply the glue evenly with a brush to the surface where the images are to go. Position and press down, expelling any trapped air bubbles by smoothing with your fingers. Both when gluing and varnishing, it is advisable to use reasonable quality brushes which will not drop bristles.

VARNISHING

Varnish finishes for découpage can be gloss, semi-gloss or matte. Most oil-based varnishes will impart a mellow look, while water-based varnishes remain clear even after many coats.

A number of layers of varnish are required for découpage, though just how many is a moot point. Between ten and twenty coats is usual, though up to sixty is not unknown. Each coat must be completely dry before you apply the next. When applying varnish, brush from one side of the piece to the other using an uninterrupted, smooth stroke. Apply each layer of varnish in an alternate direction.

SANDING

After the first ten or so coats of varnish it will be necessary to start sanding between layers of varnish. Use a sheet of medium grade sandpaper and sand in one direction with short, even-pressured strokes. Alternate the direction for subsequent layers, wiping away the dust with a soft cotton cloth and then a tack cloth each time. After about twenty coats of varnish, change to wet-and-dry sandpaper. For the last several coats use fine sandpaper. Smooth the final layer of varnish with dry steel wool, polishing in a circular motion.

GLUES AND GLUING

MAKING FLOUR PASTE

This simple glue is ideal for joining papers together and for making papier-mâché. It is non-toxic and will not make papers wrinkle if mixed to the right consistency.

To make flour paste, place two or three tablespoons of plain flour in a bowl and add a little water. Stir to make a smooth paste. Gradually add more water until the paste is the consistency of thick cream. Apply flour paste with a brush or with your fingers.

OTHER GLUES

Wallpaper paste makes an acceptable substitute for flour paste and is made by mixing the cellulose powder with water. Follow the manufacturer's instructions for use, but add powder or water to thicken or dilute the mix according to the project at hand.

Paste is suitable for joining paper to paper, or paper to cardboard, but it must be applied sparingly. PVA glue has extra strength and is ideal for gluing pieces of cardboard together, as well as for reinforcing the joints of boxes and other items made from paper or wood.

WORKING WITH PAPER

FINDING THE GRAIN

When paper is folded with the grain it will crease easily and lie flat. To test the direction of the grain of a sheet of paper or cardboard, hold it at opposite sides and bend it, then flex again in the other direction. The side which puts up the least resistance will have the grain running parallel with the line of the bend.

When gluing a sheet of paper onto a board and when cutting out pieces for use in the construction of functional objects, make sure that the grain of all the papers align with each other. This eliminates warping and gives the finished object greater strength.

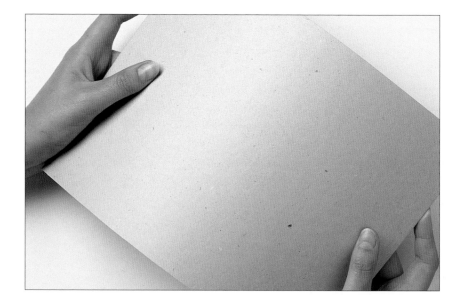

CREASING AND TEARING

Heavy papers that are difficult to fold can be scored before folding. Find the grain of the paper and place a metal ruler along the line to be creased. With a pointed instrument such as a needle, scratch a line into the surface of the paper. Fold the paper so that the scored line forms the outer side of the crease.

Many paper folding techniques involve making creases. Origami is the most obvious example. Test first for the direction of the grain if the paper is to be folded in one direction only. When making creases, lay the paper on a flat surface with the line to be folded running horizontally from left to right. Pick up the edge nearest to you and locate it at the appropriate position, then make the crease with your fingers. To make the edge sharper, run a bone folder or the edge of a ruler along the fold.

It is easier to tear a sheet of paper along the grain than against it. Make a sharp crease where you want the paper to be torn, and open the sheet out. Then, with one hand holding the paper flat on a hard surface close to the line of the crease, pull at the other side of the crease while slightly lifting the paper. If you like, you can dampen the crease with a little water first to soften the paper. The resulting tear will have a deckle-like edge.

QUILLING SHAPES

To begin any coil, insert the end of a strip of paper into the slot of the quilling tool and wind away from yourself. Other instruments such as a hat pin or toothpick can be used instead of a quilling tool if you prefer.

TIGHT COIL OR FILLER
Wind the paper strip tightly to the end, remove it from the tool and glue the end of the strip to hold the shape.

LOOSE COIL
Wind the strip to the end as for a tight roll, but before gluing, allow the coil to expand to the required size.

SCROLL
Begin making a loose coil, but stop winding before you reach the end of the strip. Release to form the scroll.

DOUBLE SCROLL
Make a scroll, starting at one end of a strip, then make a scroll in the opposite direction at the other end.

TEARDROP
Make a loose coil and glue the end. Pinch one side into a point while pulling the center towards the other end.

EYE-SHAPE
Follow the directions for making a loose coil then pinch opposite sides of the shape to form an eye.

CRESCENT
Follow the directions for making a loose coil, then gently squeeze into a semi-circle, pinching into shape.

DIAMOND
Follow the directions for making a loose coil, then gently squeeze the shape into a diamond form.

PETAL
Follow the directions for making a teardrop. As you pinch one end, gently pull it to one side to make a petal.

TOOLS AND EQUIPMENT

PAPER MAKING

MOLD

A durable frame for paper making can be constructed from pieces of wood. The size of the paper you wish to make will be determined by the inside dimensions of the frame. To make sheets of standard size paper, the inside area of the frame will need to measure 11 x 8½ inches (28 x 21.5 cm).

Select pieces of wood which measure ¾ inch (2 cm) square. Cut two 12½ inch (32 cm) long strips and two 10 inch (25.5 cm) long strips. Miter the ends of each piece to 45° angles.

Use a water-resistant wood glue to join all the mitered joints. When the glue is dry, fix staples over each of the joints for greater strength. Using a medium grade sandpaper, smooth the frame and paint it with two coats of timber-finish varnish.

Cut a 12½ x 10 inch (32 x 25.5 cm) rectangle of fine aluminum mesh. Stretch it tightly over the frame and staple down. Place the staples closely to ensure the mesh is secure.

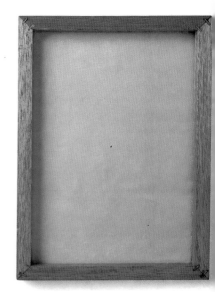

DECKLE

The deckle is a removable open frame which fits exactly over the mold. The deckle prevents the pulp from running away too quickly and gives the finished sheet the 'deckled,' or untrimmed, edge characteristic of handmade paper.

For a simple deckle, make a second frame identical to that made for the mold, omitting the mesh. Molds and deckles can also be purchased ready-made from craft suppliers.

MARBLING

TRAY

A shallow, waterproof box can be made from pieces of exterior-grade plywood. The tray should be slightly larger than the size of the sheet of paper to be marbled. A simple open box is adequate, but there are certain refinements, such as a slop trough and a drainage hole, which can make the process of marbling easier.

The following directions are for a tray with the dimensions 31½ x 19¾ inch (80 x 50 cm):

Onto ½ inch (9 mm) thick plywood measure the following pieces: one 31½ x 19¾ inch (80 x 50 cm) base, two 31½ x 2¾ inch (80 x 7 cm) sides, two 19 x 2¾ inch (48 x 7 cm) ends and one 19 x 2⅓ inch (48 x 6 cm) trough partition. Cut out the pieces, beveling one of the long edges of the trough partition to a 45° angle.

Drill a drainage hole in one corner of the base piece. (Select a cork or rubber sink plug first, then drill the hole to fit.)

Use water-resistant wood glue to join the two end pieces to the base, then the long side pieces, and clamp to dry. Apply extra glue around all the joints to ensure a waterproof seal.

Glue the trough partition across the box. Sand the tray to remove any roughness and apply three coats of marine varnish.

If you are making a tray without a slop trough, remember to reduce the length of the tray to suit the size of your paper.

SKIMMER

A narrow board, cut slightly shorter than the width of the tray, is used to clean the marbling size. A piece of skirting board which narrows at the top is suitable. Alternatively, cut a 2 inch (5 cm) wide strip of balsawood. Sand and varnish the wood to make it smooth and waterproof before use.

WASH BOARD

A wash board is inserted into the slop trough and used to lay a freshly printed sheet of paper against for rinsing.

To make a wash board, draw the base shape onto ½ inch (9 mm) thick exterior-grade plywood according to the measurements indicated in the diagram to the right. Then, onto ½ inch (9 mm) plywood, measure the following pieces: one 22 x 1¼ inch (56 x 3 cm) end strip, two 31½ x 1¼ inch (80 x 3 cm) side strips and two 2⅓ x 1¼ inch (6 x 3 cm) strips for the angled side strips. Cut out all pieces, beveling the long and short side strips where they will meet at the corners.

Using water-resistant wood glue, join the end strip to the base board, then the long and short side strips. Hold the glued joints with clamps until dry, and cover the joints with an additional line of glue.

Sand the wash board and apply three coats of marine varnish.

A block of wood placed behind the slop trough partition holds the wash board at the correct angle. The block should be approximately ¾ inch (2 cm) thick, 2⅓ inches (6 cm) wide and 6 inches (15 cm) long. Paint with varnish to seal.

22⅓ inches (58 cm)

31½ inches (80 cm)

2⅓ inches (6 cm)

3½ inches (9 cm)

19⅓ inches (49 cm)

RAKE

Make your rake to fit inside the length of the tray which you are using. Lay the wood flat and draw a line down the center of it. Along this line, mark a series of dots at 2 inch (5 cm) intervals, the first and last points being only 1 inch (2.5 cm) from either end.

Plastic hair curler pins make suitable pegs for the prongs of your rake. Their width will determine the size of the drill bit you use to make the holes. Drill the holes at the points marked and insert the pins. The fit should be fairly tight, but not so tight that they cannot be removed later should you want to alter the length of the rake or the number of prongs.

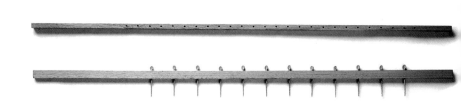

COMB

Cut two strips of ¼ inch (6 mm) thick pine, each 18½ inches long x 2⅓ inches wide (47 x 6 cm).

Draw a line down the center of one of the strips and mark a series of dots at ¼ inch (5 mm) intervals. Apply waterproof glue along the line and place long, stainless steel pins at the points marked, protruding about 1⅓ inches (3 cm).

Apply more glue over the pinheads and allow to dry. Then apply glue all over the surface and attach the other strip of wood.

WHISK

A whisk is an effective tool for applying color to the surface of the size mixture in a splattered effect. Cut a small bunch of millet straw to a length of about 8 inches (20 cm) and bind the straws together near the base with string or a rubber band. Millet straw is available at some craft stores; alternatively, a millet-straw broom can be cut to the length required.

QUILLING

QUILLING BOARD

Rolled paper strips are assembled on a quilling board prior to gluing them onto the item to be decorated. A grid facilitates the accurate spacing and measuring of the quilled shapes.

To make a quilling board, cut two or three pieces of thick cardboard to a standard page or larger. Glue together, then glue a piece of graph paper on top and cover with a sheet of adhesive plastic for protection.

A piece of tracing paper can be temporarily attached over the grid with masking tape to make a smooth surface on which to glue the pieces. Separate the quilled shapes from the paper by sliding a flat knife between them.

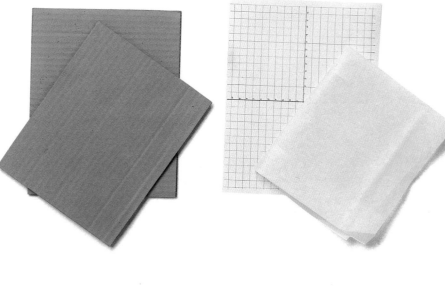

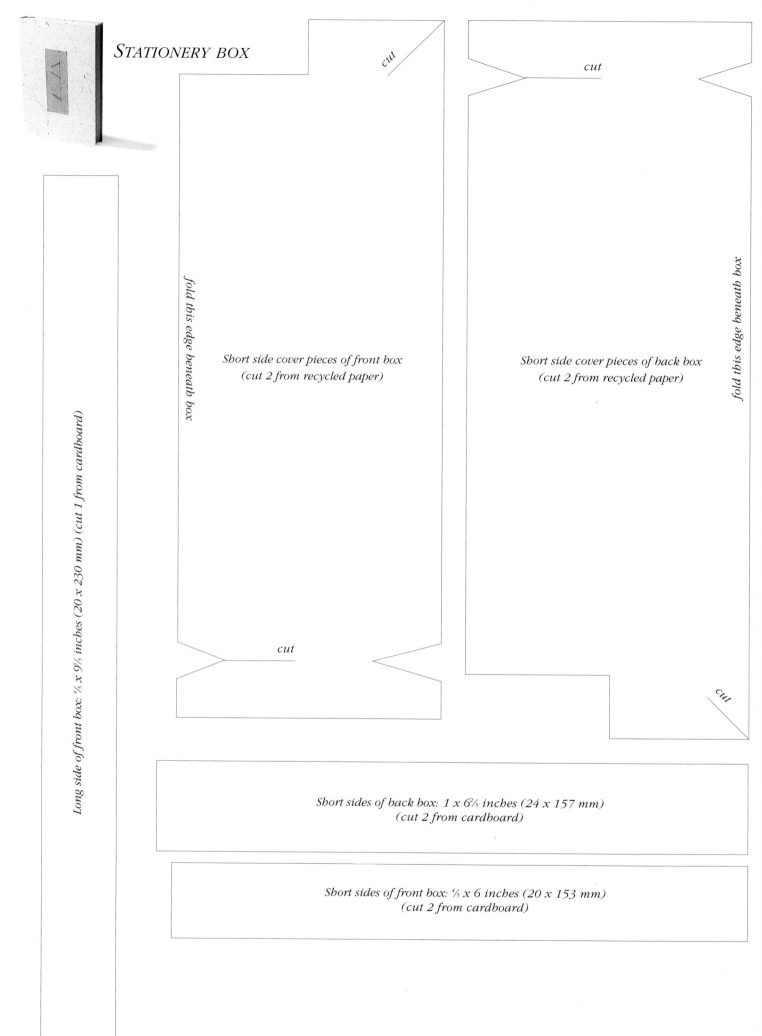

STATIONERY BOX

fold this edge beneath box

Short side cover pieces of front box
(cut 2 from recycled paper)

cut

cut

Short side cover pieces of back box
(cut 2 from recycled paper)

cut

cut

fold this edge beneath box

Long side of front box: ⅘ x 9⅖ inches (20 x 230 mm) (cut 1 from cardboard)

Short sides of back box: 1 x 6⅕ inches (24 x 157 mm)
(cut 2 from cardboard)

Short sides of front box: ⅘ x 6 inches (20 x 153 mm)
(cut 2 from cardboard)

Lining paper for base of front box: 6⅓ x 8¼ inches (160 x 210 mm) (cut 1 from recycled paper)

Lining paper for base of back box: 6⅓ x 8½ inches (160 x 220 mm) (cut 1 from recycled paper)

Base for front box: 6 x 9 inches (155 x 230 mm) (cut 1 from cardboard)

Spine: 1 x 9¾ inches (24 x 244 mm) (cut 1 from cardboard)

Long side of back box: 1 x 9⅓ inches (24 x 238 mm) (cut 1 from cardboard)

Base for back box: 6⅓ x 9⅓ inches (159 x 238 mm) (cut 1 from cardboard)

Outside front & back covers: 6⅓ x 9⅓ inches (162 x 245 mm) (cut 1 each from cardboard)

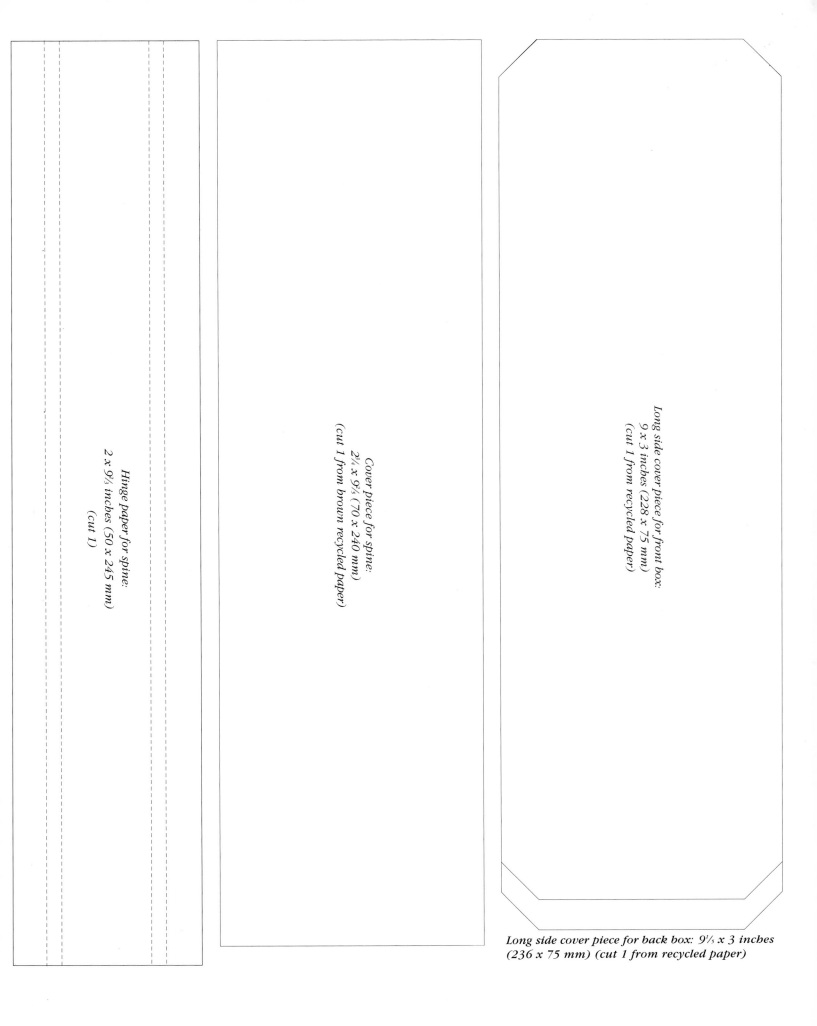

Hinge paper for spine:
2 x 9⅓ inches (50 x 245 mm)
(cut 1)

Cover piece for spine:
2¾ x 9⅗ (70 x 240 mm)
(cut 1 from brown recycled paper)

Long side cover piece for front box:
9 x 3 inches (228 x 75 mm)
(cut 1 from recycled paper)

Long side cover piece for back box: 9⅓ x 3 inches
(236 x 75 mm) (cut 1 from recycled paper)

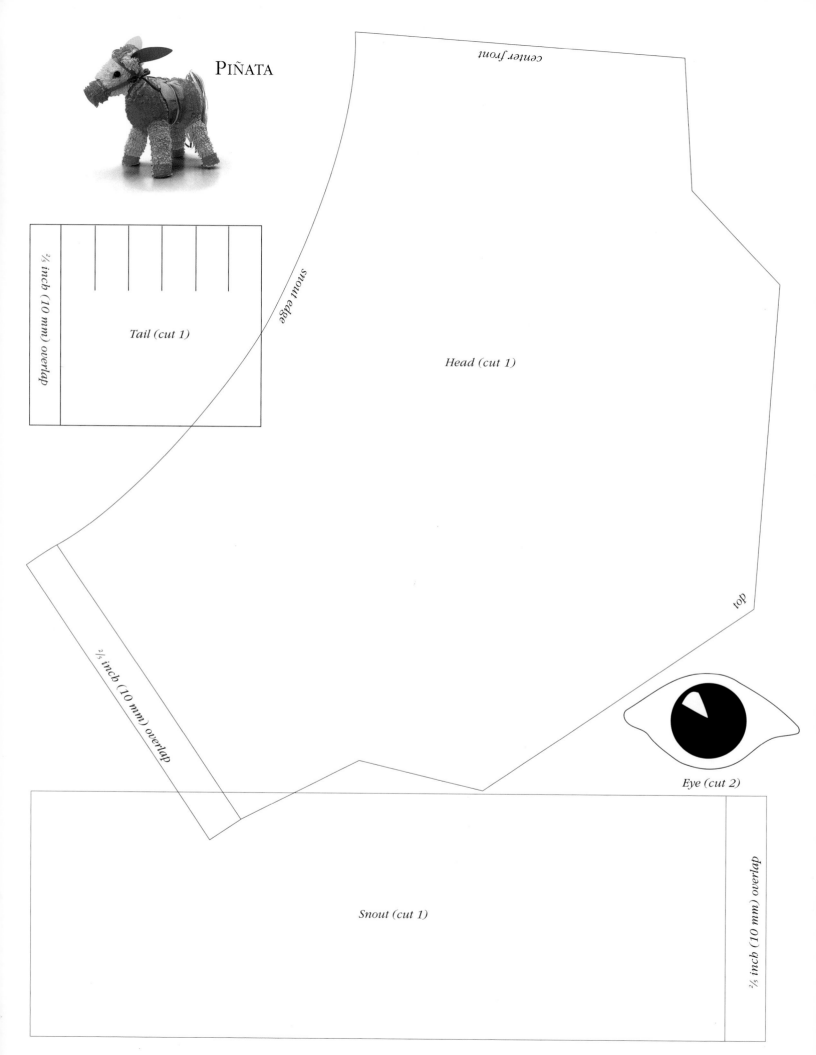

PIÑATA

Tail (cut 1)

²/₅ inch (10 mm) overlap

snout edge

center front

Head (cut 1)

top

²/₅ inch (10 mm) overlap

Eye (cut 2)

Snout (cut 1)

²/₅ inch (10 mm) overlap

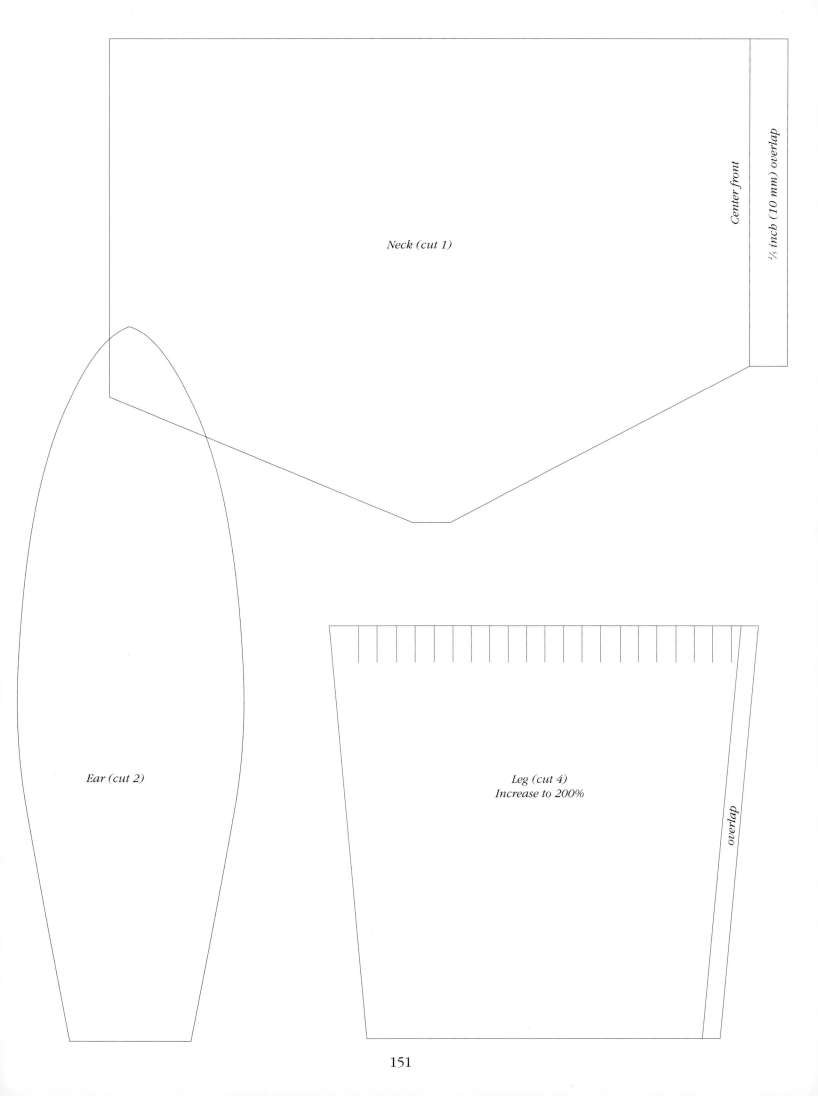

Neck (cut 1)

Center front

⅖ inch (10 mm) overlap

Ear (cut 2)

Leg (cut 4)
Increase to 200%

overlap

*Increase pattern to fit
the desired size*

SHIMADA *DOLL*

fold to back

fold to back

Obi *loop: 4 x 6 inches (100 x 150 mm) (cut 1)*

fold to back

fold to back

Obi *bow: 4 x 7⅓ inches (100 x 200 mm) (cut 1)*

fold to back
fold to back

Obi *wrap for body: 4 x 6 inches (100 x 150 mm) (cut 1)*

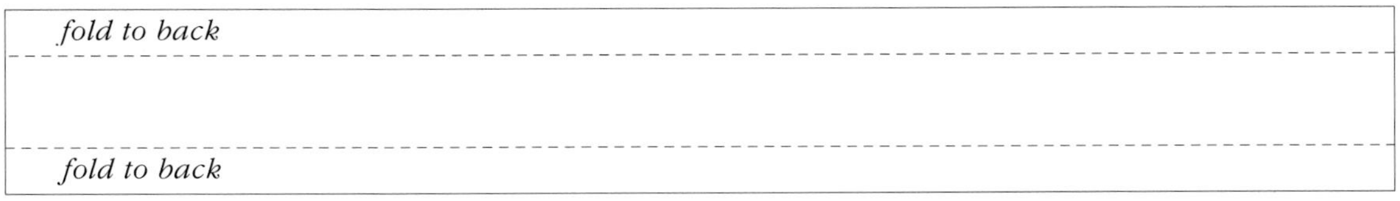
fold to back
fold to back

Obi *sash: 4/5 x 6 inches (20 x 150 mm) (cut 1)*

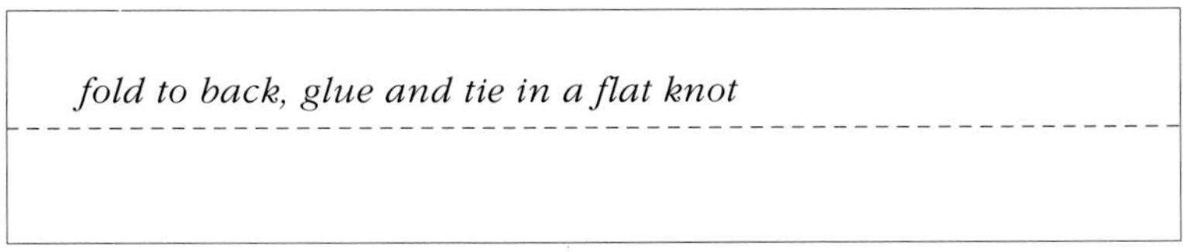
fold to back, glue and tie in a flat knot

Hair bow: 4/5 x 4 inches (20 x 100 mm) (cut 1)

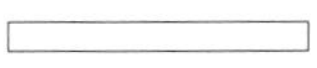

Hat pin

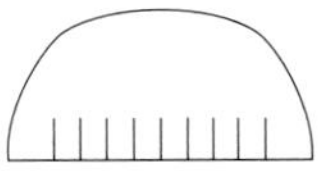

Comb: 4/5 x 4/5 inches (20 x 20 mm)

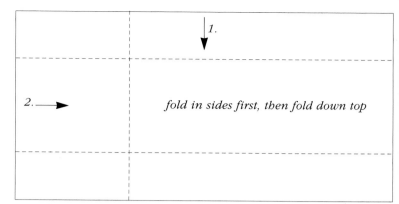

Front hair piece: 2 x 4 inches (50 x 100 mm) (cut 1)

*Face piece: 2¾ x 6 inches
(70 x 150 mm) (cut 1)*

Main hair piece: 4 x 9⅘ inches (100 mm x 250 mm) (cut 1)

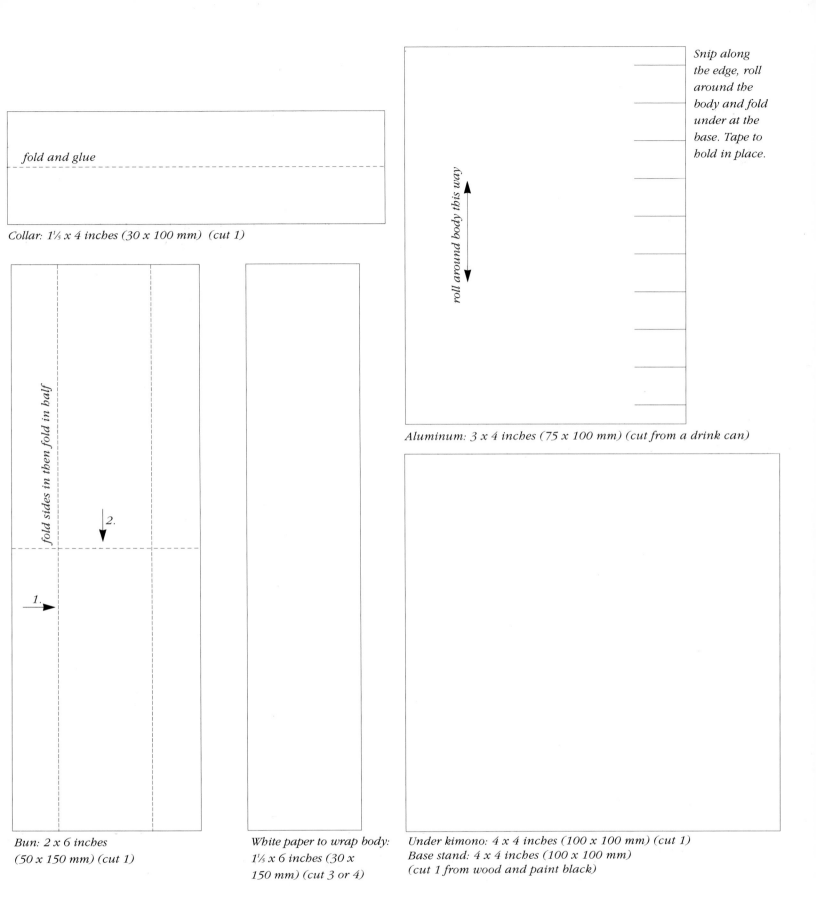

fold and glue

Collar: 1⅕ x 4 inches (30 x 100 mm) (cut 1)

fold sides in then fold in half

1.

2.

roll around body this way

Snip along the edge, roll around the body and fold under at the base. Tape to hold in place.

Aluminum: 3 x 4 inches (75 x 100 mm) (cut from a drink can)

Bun: 2 x 6 inches
(50 x 150 mm) (cut 1)

White paper to wrap body:
1⅕ x 6 inches (30 x
150 mm) (cut 3 or 4)

Under kimono: 4 x 4 inches (100 x 100 mm) (cut 1)
Base stand: 4 x 4 inches (100 x 100 mm)
(cut 1 from wood and paint black)

4. Fold to the back

pleat

1. fold to the back

2. fold to the back again

3. fold to the front

pleat when placed around the body

Upper kimono: 4 x 7 inches (100 x 180 mm) (cut 1)

Align the plain and patterned lower kimono pieces in the position shown and glue together

As a guide, this depth should equal 8½ inches (220 mm) →

Lower patterned kimono (cut 1)

Plain lower kimono (cut 1)

*O*RIGAMI *BOX*

Base - cut squares to a size of 11⅘ x 11⅘ inches (300 x 300 mm)
Cut 1 from blue razak *paper and 1 from patterned* chiogami *paper*
Broken lines indicate folds

Lid - cut squares to a size of 11⅕ x 11⅕ inches (300 x 300 mm)
Cut 1 from blue razak *paper and 1 from red* momijami *paper*
Broken lines indicate folds

WASHI CHIGIRI-E

top

*Increase pattern to 135% to fit the
mountboard used in this project*

162

PAPIER-MÂCHÉ TRAY

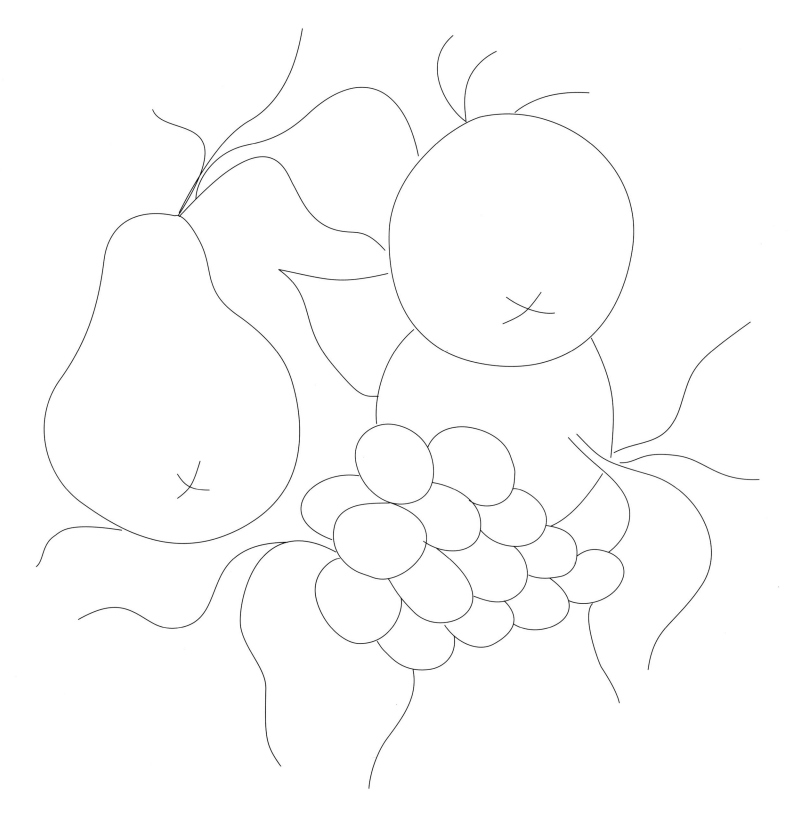

*Increase pattern to fit the finished
size of the papier-mâché tray*

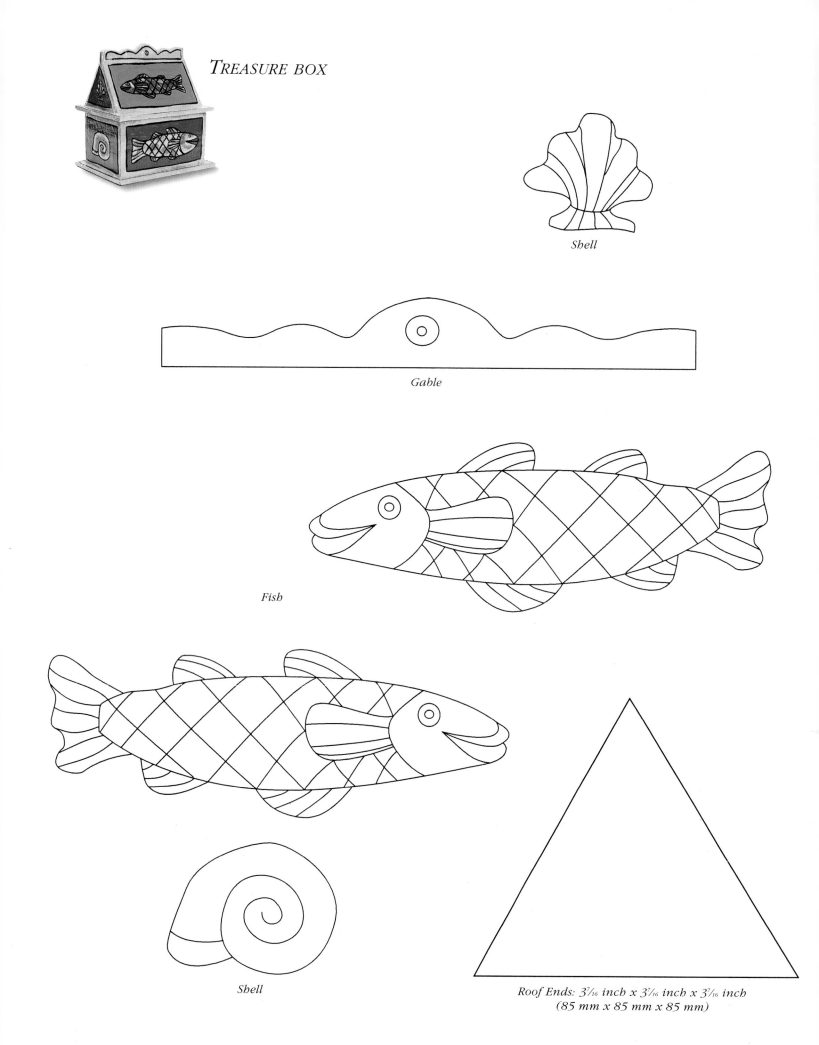

TREASURE BOX

Shell

Gable

Fish

Shell

*Roof Ends: 3⁷⁄₁₆ inch x 3⁷⁄₁₆ inch x 3⁷⁄₁₆ inch
(85 mm x 85 mm x 85 mm)*

Inner Lid: 5¼ x 3⅓ inches (135 x 80 mm)

Roof Sides: 6 x 3¼ inches (150 x 85 mm)

Roof Base: 6¼ x 5 inches (170 x 125 mm)

Box Base Long Side: 3⅓ x 6 inches (80 mm x 150 mm)

Box Base Short Side: 3⅓ x 4 inches (80 x 100 mm)

Box Base: 6¼ x 5⅛ inches (170 x 130 mm)

SHELF LINER

fold to back

SILHOUETTE

*This pattern can be enlarged or reduced
to fit the size of the frame to be used*

QUILLED BOX

CHINESE LANTERN

CHINESE PAPERCUT

GLOSSARY

Mexican alebridge

alebridge: Fantastical papier-mâché creatures made in Mexico.

alum: A mordant, or color fixative. Available in three crystalline salts, it is dissolved in water and applied to paper prior to marbling.

amate: A primitive paper made from the bark of mulberry and fig trees, it is the Mexican precursor of modern fiber pulp papers.

antiquing: The application of paint and a medium to give an article an aged and mellow appearance.

baroque: A decorative style developed in Italy in the sixteenth century, characterized by the use of asymmetry and lavish ornamentation.

binding: The fabric or paper strip that protects and adorns the edge of a book.

bone folder: A knife-like instrument made from bone which is used to form a smooth crease when folding a sheet of paper.

bouquet design: One of many marbling patterns, the bouquet design is made on a nonpareil background and raked in a zigzag pattern to produce a design which resembles the plumage of a peacock.

Boys' Day: A Japanese celebration held on the last day of spring and celebrated with the display of *koi nobori*, paper carp streamers which are hung from poles and which symbolize courage and perseverance.

caustic soda: An alkali that helps to break down plant fibers during boiling. Also known as soda ash, it is chemically activated when added to water.

Chinoiserie: A style of European art, popular in the eighteenth century, based on the imitation of motifs from Chinese art.

comb: One of the two main tools used in marbling to manipulate the paint surface, the other being the rake. The comb has fine teeth spaced closely together.

couching: The process of transferring a newly formed sheet of paper from the screen to a bed of damp felt or blanket and draining excess water away.

deckle: The rectangular wooden frame that fits over the paper making mold, used for forming sheets of paper.

deckle edge: The distinctive irregular edge of handmade paper.

découpage: The process of decorating an object with an arrangement of cut-out paper images. Many layers of varnish are applied on top of the images to disguise the cut edges and give the impression of a single piece of artwork.

Dolls' Festival: Also called *hina-matsuri*, or Girls' Day, this Japanese festival celebrates girls' growth and health and centers on the display of elaborate paper dolls.

embedding: The process of incorporating foreign materials into a sheet of paper for a decorative effect.

endpaper: A sheet of strong paper, half of which is pasted on to the inside cover of a book, the other half forming the flyleaf, the first or last blank sheet.

filigree: A term used to describe ornamental work of scrolls and arabesques. Filigree is usually associated with metal work, but is also associated with paper rolling, being another name for quilling.

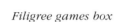

Filigree games box

Fourdrinier machine: The first paper making machine, invented in France in 1799, but set up in England in 1804 by the Fourdrinier brothers. The machine consisted of a belt which traveled through a vat of pulp to produce a continuous length of paper.

gesso: A thick, white undercoat used as a primer.

Girls' Day: See Dolls' festival.

grain: The direction in which the fibers of a sheet of paper lie. In machine-made papers, fibers are vibrated to lie in line with the direction of travel of the belt.

grotesque: A découpage style which uses classic Greek and Roman images in a comic and outrageous manner.

Hollander Beater: A Dutch machine designed in the seventeenth century to shred rags and ropes, making them suitable for making into paper.

huang-hua: Brightly colored Chinese papercuts which are used as decorations for windows. The name comes from northern China and literally means 'window flowers.'

Huang-hua *papercut*

Judases: Papier-mâché figures representing skeletons and skulls. They are filled with fireworks and exploded during the Holy Week celebrations in Mexico.

kimono: A loosely fitting robe made from silk or cotton. This traditional Japanese garment was brought to Japan by Buddhist monks from China some time in the eighth century.

koi norobi: Streamers made from paper or silk in the shape of carp and hoisted to the top of a tall pole or attached to the roof of a house as part of the Boys' Day celebrations in Japan.

kozo: A kind of Japanese tree, the bark of which is used to make paper.

lacquering: The process of applying varnish, traditionally obtained from the sap of a type of tree found in Japan and China.

Liebesbrief: A papercut love letter popularized in the mid-1700s by Johannes Uhlman, a young Pennsylvanian who sent his lover an intricately cut design covered with hearts, flowers and love verses.

manekineko: A beckoning cat figurine often found displayed at the front of Japanese shops to entice customers and bring prosperity.

marbling: A painted finish achieved by floating colored paints on a thickened liquid then lifting them off onto a sheet of paper. The craft is named for its resemblance to marbled stone.

measuring box: A small square box, called *masu*, usually made of Japanese cypress, is used for measuring rice and for drinking Japanese wine.

milles fleurs: Literally meaning 'a thousand flowers', this term refers to the late eighteenth century découpage style which uses busy, all-over patterns of paper images.

mineral turpentine: A volatile spirit, originally derived from pine resin, used as a solvent for oil-based substances.

Marbled lamp shades

mon-kiri: A Japanese tradition of paper cutting, dating back to the eleventh century. The word translates as 'crest-cutting' and is derived from the ancient practice of cutting designs to make family emblems or crests which commonly appeared as textile designs.

mordant: A substance used in dyeing to fix the color. Alum, derived from the word aluminum, is the most common mordant applied to papers.

mold: The shape or object on which a cast is formed, usually in a fluid or plastic state.

Mould and deckle

mold and deckle: The equipment for making paper, consisting of two rectangular wooden frames that fit together. The mold has a wire mesh attached to it for straining the paper pulp.

mountboard: A good quality cardboard, used mostly for picture framing, but ideal for paper making.

Necmeddin Okyay: A Turk who promoted the style of marbling which involves manipulating paints on a size surface to produce pictures rather than abstract patterns.

nonpareil: One of the most popular marbling patterns, and one which forms the base for a number of other marbling designs. It is achieved by a set of simple raking and combing motions.

ningyo: The Japanese word for doll. A great variety of dolls are made in Japan, many of them from paper.

Origami box

obi: A broad sash tied in a decorative bow at the back, worn with a Japanese kimono.

origami: The Japanese art of folding paper into shapes representing animals, flowers and other objects, with boxes being a popular design.

overprinting: A term used in marbling to describe the process of marbling a sheet of paper more than once to create a multi-layered effect.

ox gall: An oily substance extracted from the gall bladder of cows, ox gall is added to water-based marbling paints to enable them to spread and float on the liquid size.

papel picado: The Mexican craft of cutting layers of tissue paper with a knife to form lacy designs which are traditionally hung up on strings to help celebrate All Souls' Day.

paper pulping: The process of shredding paper, combining it with water and blending to a pulp for use in paper making and papier-mâché.

papier-mâché: Paper strips or pulp combined with glue and molded into shape. When dry, papier-mâché forms a hard, light material which is ideal for decorating with a painted finish.

papyrus: A writing material traditionally prepared from thin strips of the pith of the papyrus plant which are laid together, soaked, pressed and dried.

Mexican papier-mâché doll

parchment: Thick paper resembling the writing material prepared from the skin of goats and sheep, traditionally used for writing and book binding.

petroleum jelly: A soft, greasy substance obtained from petroleum, it is used as a protective covering and a lubricant.

piñata: Mexican toy made from clay or papier-mâché which is filled with sweets, suspended from a pole and broken by children to reveal the presents inside.

pulp: Any fiber derived from plants, recycled paper or even animal hair that has been macerated.

quilling: The craft of rolling narrow paper strips and standing them on end to form decorative patterns.

rake: A marbling tool with widely spaced teeth, used for patterning paints on the surface of the size. The rake is pulled in both directions for most marbling patterns.

rococo: A style of European art, architecture and decoration of the eighteenth century, distinguished by its ornate use of scrolls and curves.

scherenschnitte: The traditional German style of paper cutting characterized by an abundance of plant and animal motifs. The intricate papercuts are made with scissors or knives.

sheaf: A bundle of papers.

Shimada doll: A type of Japanese doll constructed from paper. The hairstyle lends the name to the doll, elaborate chignons being fashionable amongst women in the city of Shimada in the Edo period.

silhouette: An outline drawing, uniformly filled in with black, popularized by the Frenchman August Edouart but named after Etienne de Silhouette, an eighteenth century politician renowned for his severe economizing—hence the association of his name with this stark form of portraiture.

sizing: The application of weak, glue-like substances to papers to make them stronger and less absorbent.

size: A thickening agent mixed with water to assist marbling paints to float. The most common sizing agent is carrageenan, a derivative of seaweed, which causes the water to thicken to a gelatinous consistency.

skimmer: A strip of wood used to skim the surface of the sized liquid contained within the marbling tray to rid it of dust and air bubbles.

suminagashi: The earliest form of marbling, first practiced in Japan in the twelfth century. Literally meaning 'ink floating,' *suminagashi* designs are made by dropping colors onto water and gently blowing or combing them into patterns.

trompe l'oeil: French for 'trick the eye,' the term refers to a style of painting or découpage which seeks to counterfeit reality.

Turkish marbling: A style of marbling, developed in Turkey, wherein pictures are formed on the sized liquid by the careful manipulation of paints with a probe.

Turkish marbled design

vat: Used in paper making, a vat contains the water in which the paper or fiber pulp is suspended, ready for collecting on a mold and deckle.

wash board: A frame with a smooth wooden surface which is inserted into the slop trough of a marbling tray and is used for washing size off a marbled sheet.

washi: Japanese paper. It is available in a range of textures and colors, but all *washi* papers are characterized by a thinness and pliancy.

watermark: A translucent figure or design, impressed during the paper making process, which is visible when a sheet of paper is held up to the light. It is formed by sewing fine wire thread onto the mold.

whisk: Used in marbling to splatter paint evenly over a sized liquid surface. Whisks are made from small bunches of broom straw tied together.

wycinanki: The Polish word for papercut designs. Traditionally made by peasants, *wycinanki* designs are cut from single sheets of colored paper.

Scherenschnitte *papercut*

CONTRIBUTORS

Marion Elliot is one of Britain's leading papier-mâché artists. She has contributed to many books, as well as writing her own, and her work has often been exhibited. Marion specializes in original paper sculptures and accessories.

Amanda Ho is multi-talented in papercraft, but découpage is her speciality. Teaching, writing and researching occupy this Australian craftswoman's working time, as well as creating unique, internationally commissioned découpage pieces.

Melinda Lai was schooled in Japan, and it was there that she developed an interest in origami. Due to her father's influence as a merchant for Japanese papers, Melinda developed a close affinity with the medium. Her beautiful origami creations are proof of this.

Sandra Levy has contributed significantly to the appreciation of *scherenschnitte* in Australia. She began paper cutting in the early eighties, after a visit to America, and now teaches from her studio. Sandra's work has been published in many journals.

Anne Redman is a prominent Australian quiller who designs and sells quilling worksheets. In 1992 she launched the *Australian Quillers' Quarterly*, a journal for the exchange of quilling ideas. Anne's work has been exhibited widely.

Brenda Rhodes is an English craftswoman with a long list of quilling credits to her name. A member of the Quilling Guild, in which she has held a number of offices, Brenda has written, lectured and broadcast extensively on the craft.

Juliette Rubensohn developed an appreciation for handmade paper in 1985 while working as a translator in Japan. This led to a study tour of Japanese paper making workshops. Returning to Australia she became apprenticed as a paper maker and now works with a Sydney paper making enterprise, Primrose Park.

Margo Snape was a graphic artist and calligrapher when she was introduced to marbling in 1984. Margo now works exclusively as a marbler and is much in demand as a leading craftswoman in this field. She has traveled all over the world to research the craft and collect marbled papers.

Peter Travis is a celebrated artist-craftsman and a noted colorist whose kites have achieved worldwide fame. Peter is the second living person to have been elected into the Hall of Fame of the World Kite Museum in America. As well as exhibiting his work, he also collects ethnic folk kites.

Kazuko Willy is one of only a few artists in Australia practicing the craft of *washi chigiri-e*. She recently visited Japan to learn more about the art of paper tearing, and plans to make a business of her hobby.

INDEX

advanced projects
    Chinese kite 118-121
    quilled box 110-113
    Shimada doll 70-73
    stationery box 16-19
    Turkish marbling 46-49
alebridges 29, 31
alum 137
amate 9, 29-31, 96

baroque 55
beginner projects
    making paper 12-15
    oil marbled compendium 50-53
    origami box 74-77
    papel picado placemats 36-37
    paper pulp bowl 24-27
    shelf liner 102-103
    silhouette 104-105
    washi chigiri-e 78-81
binding 11, 22
bouquet marbling design 42, 44-45

carp streamers 67
carrageenan size 137
Chinese papercraft 95, 97, 115-127
    kites 115, 118-121
    lanterns 67, 115-116, 122-125
Chinoiserie 56, 83
couching 13-14, 135
crackling 111
crazy quilt découpage 56

Day of the Dead 30-31
découpage 6, 54-65
    cutting 60
    gluing 59-60, 64, 138
    sanding 61, 64, 139
    sealing 59, 61, 138
    sponging 65
    varnishing 61, 64, 138

Edo period 70
embedding 9, 11, 22, 26-27
endpapers 23

Festival of Ascending on High 115
fiber pulping 10, 12-13, 18, 134
filigree (see quilling)
woven 108
flax 12-13
flour paste 17, 139
Fourdrinier machine 9
fringing 108

gluing 139
grotesque style 56

hina ningyo 68
Hollander Beater 9
Holy Week 29, 31
huang-hua 96, 115

intermediate projects
    Chinese lantern 122-125
    Chinese papercut 126-127
    découpage book box 58-61
    découpage vase 62-65
    handmade paper book 20-23
    Mexican piñata 32-35
    papier-mâché tray 86-89
    papier-mâché treasure box 90-93
    scherenschnitte 98-101
    watercolor marbling 42-49

Japanese papercraft 66-81
Judases 29

Lantern Festival 115
lashing 120

manekineko 85
marbling 6, 39-53
    tools 143-145
    making size 137
    mixing colors 136-137
materials 132-133
measuring box 74-77
Mexican papercraft 6, 28-37, 96
milles fleurs 56
mon-kiri 96
mold and deckle 13-14, 142
molds 10, 83-85

North American papercraft
    tradition 6, 95-96, 107

origami 6, 67-68, 74-77
Okyay, Necmeddin 46

paper
    caring for 129
    creasing 140
    cutting 129
    dyeing 25
    grain 17, 128, 140
    tearing 22, 140
    types 130-131
    weight 128-129

paper cutting 6, 29, 31, 36-37, 94-105, 115-117
paper making 8-27, 134-135
paper pulp 10, 12-14, 24-27, 134
papier-mâché 6, 29-33, 69, 82-93
papel picado 6, 29, 31, 36-37, 96
piñata 29, 32-35
Polish paper cutting 95, 97

quilling board 111, 145
quilling 6, 107-113
    board 145
    shapes 141
    tool 107, 109

rococo 55, 62

scherenschnitte 95-96, 98-101
silhouette 95, 104-105
sizing 15, 135
skimmer 143
Spring Festival 115
suminagashi 39

transferring patterns 129
trompe l'oeil 56
three-dimensional découpage 57
Turkish marbling 39, 46-49

Victorian age 55

washi chigiri-e 67, 78-81
watercolor marbling 50-53, 136
watermarks 10
wycinanki 95-96

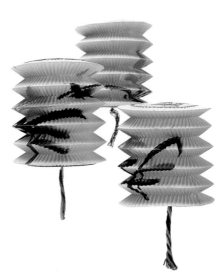

ACKNOWLEDGEMENTS

PHOTO CREDITS

front cover, 1, 3, 15, 18, 19, 94, 104, 118, 126, 128-137, 140, 142-145, all tool shots Andrew Payne; 2, 6, 9, 10-11, 22, 24-27, 38, 84-85, 90-93, 97, 106, 107-109 Mathew Ward; 4-5 Andre Martin; 6, 28-30 Ignacio Urquiza; 30 Andre Martin; 31 Ignacio Urquiza; 32-35, 54-61 Andre Martin; 66 Obremski/The Image Bank; 67 Lou Jones/The Image Bank; 82 The Royal Collection, Her Majesty The Queen; 83 by courtesy of the Board Of Trustees of the Victoria & Albert Museum; 92 Marie-Helene Grabman; all other shots, including step-by-steps, Adam Bruzzone.

Projects were designed and completed by:

Marion Elliot - papier-mâché treasure box on 90
Susan Grey - silhouette on 104, painting and making card for chinese paper cut on 128
Amanda Ho - découpage book box on 58, découpage vase on 62
Vicki James - mexican pinata on 32
Melinda Lei - shimada doll on 70, origami box on 74
Sandra Levy - scherenschnitte on 98, shelf liner on 102, fish design for chinese paper cut on 128
Debi McCulloch - handmade book on 20, papel picado placemats on
36, oil marbled compendium construction on 50, papier-mâché tray construction on 86, chinese lantern on 124
Jacqui Oldfield - paper pulp bowl on 24
Anne Redman - quilled box on 112
Juliette Rubonsohn - making paper on 12, stationery box on 16
Margo Snape - watercolor marbling on 42, turkish marbling on 46, oil marbled paper on 50
Peter Travis - chinese kite on 120
Katsuko Willy - washi chigiri-e on 78

Special thanks to Margo Snape and Juliette Rubonsohn for all their extra help and their precious time.

Sincere thanks to those who gave their expertise, loaned pieces and supplied materials:

Karin Besijn for allowing us the use of her shot on 8
Yvonne Chambers for illustrations on 10-11, 30-31, 40-41, 56-57, 68-6984-8596-97, 108-109, 116-117
Chinese Gardens at Darling Harbour for locations on 114, 120, 124, 126
Michael Clonaris for origami pieces on 9, 67, 68
Compton Marbling for location, pieces and tools on 2, 38, 40,
Country Form for table and chairs on 36
Corso De Fiori for locations and pieces on 20, 70, terracotta pot on 46
Mary-Anne Danaher for styling on 12, 42, 70, 78
Julia Edworthy for illustrations on 89, artwork on papier-mâché tray on 86
Marion Elliot for the papier-mâché pieces on 84
Amanda Ho for découpage papers on 5, découpage pieces on 54-57
Home & Garden for glasses on 36, cupid stand on 62
Marie-Helene Grabman for use of transparency on 95
Inca Gallery for amate papercuts on 29
Interente for paper flowers on 30
Japan Cultural Center for advice and translations, paper lantern on 68, papier-mâché tigers on 69, papier-mâché cats on 85
De-Arne King of Paper Capers, Sydney (02) 964 9471 for assistance and advice on hand made paper
Sandra Levy for papercuts on 95-97, locations on 98, 102, 104
Hannah Levy for papercut on 94
Mexican Backyard for cutlery on 36
Amy Miller for découpage plates on 57
Jacqui Oldfield for pulp bowls on 10
Brenda Rhodes for quilling pieces on 106-109
Juliette Rubensohn for watermark on 10
Margo Snape for marbled papers on 5, 39, for marbling tools and papers on 12, ornament and books 39
Timucin Tanarslan for Turkish marbled prints on 39, 40
Peter Travis for fan on 115, kites on 115, 116, 117
Dominque Vasseur for quilled posy on 6, 108
Wills Quills for papers on 66, 67, chinese character on lantern on 126

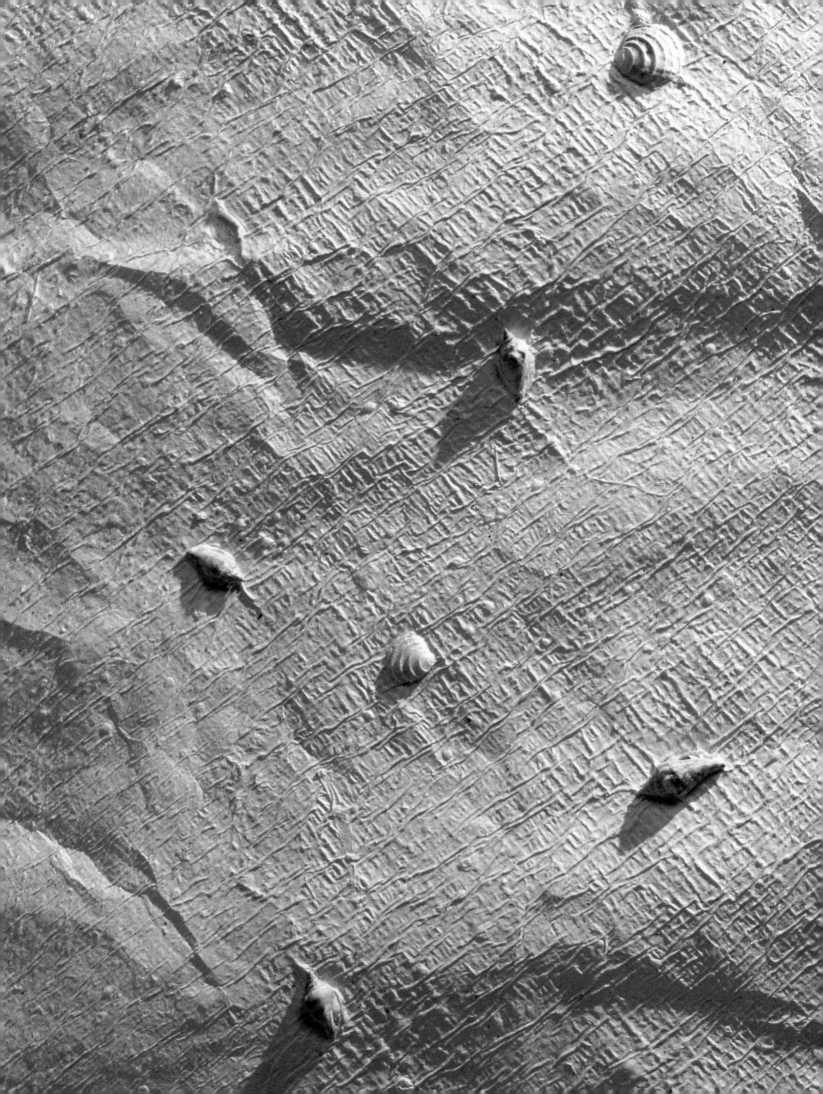